MINISTRY IN THE CHURCH

André Lemaire

Ministry in the Church

Translated by C. W. Danes

LONDON

SPCK

First published in French 1974
with the title
Les ministères dans L'Église
by Éditions du Centurion, Paris

© Éditions du Centurion 1974

First published in English 1977
SPCK
Holy Trinity Church
Marylebone Road
London NW1 4DU

Translation
© The Society for Promoting Christian Knowledge 1977

79022010

262.14
L541

Printed in Great Britain by
Bocardo & Church Army Press Ltd., Oxford

ISBN 0 281 02979 2

CONTENTS

ACKNOWLEDGEMENTS

Thanks are due to the following for permission to quote from copyright sources:

The Reverend Walter M. Abbott, S.J. and The America Press: *The Documents of Vatican II*, edited by Walter M. Abbott, S.J.*

Fortress Press: *Luther's Works*, volume 44, edited by J. Atkinson.

Oxford University Press: *Documents of the Christian Church*, selected and edited by H. Bettenson.

S.C.M. Press Ltd and The Westminster Press: *Early Christian Fathers*, Volume i, The Library of Christian Classics, newly translated and edited by Cyril C. Richardson. Published in the USA by The Westminster Press, 1953; *Early Latin Theology*, Volume v, The Library of Christian Classics, translated and edited by S.L. Greenslade. Published in the USA by The Westminster Press, 1956.

The Society for Promoting Christian Knowledge: *The Apostolic Tradition of St Hippolytus of Rome*, edited and translated by G. Dix, revised by H. Chadwick.

Biblical quotations are from the Revised Standard Version of the Bible, copyrighted 1946, 1952, © 1971, 1973 by the Division of Christian Education of the National Council of the Churches of Christ in the USA, and are used by permission.

*In the quotations from *The Documents of Vatican II*, the italics are those of the present author.

INTRODUCTION

'Crisis in the Ministry', 'crisis of vocations', 'the end of the full-time clergy', 'we are moving towards a priestless Church', all these phrases which are current nowadays and which people sometimes use as book titles cannot but disturb Christian thought. Can the Church do without priests/bishops? What is the place of the hierarchy in the Church? What is the fundamental role of the Christian ministry?

The question is important because we instinctively link the fate of the Church with that of its leaders. In the press or on the radio, when anyone uses the word 'Church' in connection with this or that problem, the word most frequently refers to declarations of the Pope, of bishops, or of priests. Of course, if the Pope and the bishops are the leaders of the Church, then by their sole authority they involve and represent the whole Christian people. Yet isn't there here a trace of 'clericalism'? Is not the Church first and foremost God's people in its entirety, and are not all Christians 'the Church'? In the end, is not the hierarchy a clerical invention?

All these questions enable us to see clearly that a deepened Christian reflection on the place of ministry in the Church is necessary, nowadays more than ever before. Indeed, behind all these present questionings we glimpse the fundamental question: What sort of Church did Jesus found? What is the ministerial function in God's plan? We want to try to answer this question, not by any ready-made answer but by

1

shedding light on it through an inquiry which will lead us to the scriptural texts and the traditions of the Church.

In accordance with this intention, we are first going to present the New Testament evidence, in the light of the advances made by some of the latest exegetical and historical studies. Given the 'canonical' value of this evidence, we shall study it in detail. Then we shall try to grasp how it has been 'lived out' — the experience of the Church through twenty centuries of her existence, drawing out in particular, from that history, the theory which has been spun about Christian ministries and the concrete fashion in which they have been exercised. After all this summing-up, which comes to us as the living memory of the Church, we shall try to grasp and formulate in the language of our own times the Christian idea of ministry and the fundamental role of the ministers in the plan of God. Finally, we shall touch on some unresolved problems which bear on the future of the ministry and on which the Church must reflect in the immediate future.

1

THE NEW TESTAMENT

The inspired witness of the New Testament about the Christian ministry has too often been interpreted differently simply because the exegete was a member of a Catholic or of a Protestant community. The advance of exegesis and of ecumenical dialogue today allows us to understand the sacred text in a more objective fashion. In order to do this, we need to put it into its literary and ecclesial context, to try to comprehend the life and problems of those first Christian communities which the Acts of the Apostles describe for us, and to whom the apostle Paul wrote his letters. In addition, we are, first of all, going to try to grasp the evolution and the diversity of the ministry during this period of a little less than a century. Having in this way resituated the varied ministries of the New Testament in their historical context, we shall be able to search for the fundamental aims and meanings of the New Testament ministry, particularly in the gospel evidence. Finally, we shall analyse some concrete aspects of the life of ministers.

A glance at history

The period we are to study extends over a little less than a century. The historian can discern four principal stages in the birth and development of the primitive Church: 1. The ministry of Jesus (c. AD 27–30); 2. The 'primitive' community of Jerusalem (c. AD 30 –43); 3. The 'apostolic' period (c. AD 43–65); 4. The period of 'evangelists and pastors' (c. AD 65–95).

Each of these stages marks a new direction in the life of the Church and in the organization of its ministries.

After his baptism by John the Baptist, Jesus preached to the crowds the coming of the Kingdom of God and the conversion necessary for its acceptance. This proclamation, like John's, was addressed to every Israelite, whatever his social class, to whatever religious grouping he belonged. Yet step by step there grew up a more restricted group of 'disciples': a certain number of keen listeners met one another regularly at the Master's feet, and it is they whom Jesus calls to leave their work in order to follow him (cf. Mark 1. 16-20). From then on, these disciples accompany Jesus in all his travels, which allows the Master to give them more systematic and detailed instruction than that of the speeches to crowds in towns and villages he visits. This group of disciples who have left their work to follow Jesus formed a community of 'living gifts' to him; more prosaically, Luke notes that several women helped this group from their own resources (Luke 8. 2-3). It is within the membership of this inner group of disciples that the calling of the Twelve takes place.

The expression 'the Twelve' belongs to the oldest sources of the Gospels. The formula 'one of the Twelve' used to designate Judas in the Passion-narratives is, for the historian, in itself a proof that the existence of this group of Twelve goes back to the earthly ministry of Jesus. More precisely, the Synoptic tradition (Matthew, Mark, Luke) is unanimous in placing the institution of this group within the framework of Jesus's Galilean ministry. But the vocabulary used by Matthew and Luke to refer to them must not mislead us; the Twelve are not 'apostles', and the expression 'the twelve apostles' is indicative of the turn of speech at the end of the first century, when these great figures

4

of the past have already disappeared.

Why choose a group of twelve men and why indicate them simply by the title 'the Twelve'? For Jesus's disciples, brought up on the tradition of the Old Testament, the meaning was clear. Jesus had chosen a group of twelve men to be leaders of the twelve tribes of Israel. Jesus himself confirms this function of the Twelve in a typically Palestinian saying:

> Truly, I say to you, in the new world, when the Son of man shall sit on his glorious throne, you who have followed me will also sit on twelve thrones, judging the twelve tribes of Israel (Matt. 19.28; Luke 22.28-30).

In this saying of Jesus's, the act of 'judging' must be understood in its biblical meaning: to judge is to decide, to command, to exercise the power of a ruler. The meaning of this proclamation of Jesus is therefore very precise, and the Twelve understood it perfectly. When Jesus is recognized as the messianic king, the Twelve will be his 'ministers'. We understand then why some among the Twelve jostled to get the best jobs — we might say the most important ministries — thus provoking the others' jealousy (Mark 10.35-40).

Having thus detailed the future responsibility of the Twelve, Jesus prepares them for it during the period of the Galilean ministry. According to Mark 3.14, they were 'to be with him, and to be sent out to preach'; before they became the ministers in the kingdom of God, Jesus expects the Twelve to be its preachers and sends them 'two by two' (Mark 6.7) through the villages of Galilee to speak to the 'lost sheep of the house of Israel' (Matt. 10.6). When their mission is over, they come back to Jesus and give him an account of what they have done and taught (Mark 6.30).

This preaching by the Twelve did not last long. For the rest of the time, the Twelve seem to have been continually with Jesus. We see them listening to his teaching in parables (Mark 4.10) and going away with Jesus into the region of Caesarea (Mark 8.27; cf. John 6.67,68). It is to them that Jesus foretells his Passion (Mark 10.32; Matt. 20.17) and teaches that leaders must serve (Mark 9.35; 10.41-45); and it is in their company that he goes up to Jerusalem and celebrates his last meal (Mark 11.11; 14,17). After the death of Judas, 'one of the Twelve', the group finds itself reduced to eleven; and it is to these that the risen Jesus appears; tradition is unanimous on this point even if the details differ (cf. Matt. 28.16; Mark 16.14; Luke 24.9,33; John 20.19,24,26; 1 Cor. 15.5).

In this company of twelve Simon, nicknamed Cephas (= Peter) by Jesus himself, is unarguably the leader (Matt. 16.17-19). Peter is the spokesman of the Twelve and puts into words the group's positive or negative reactions. It is he who proclaims that Jesus is Messiah (Mark 8.29), but it is he also who refuses a suffering Messiah (Mark 8.32; cf. John 13.8). It is he who denies Jesus during the Passion and who repents (Mark 14.66-72). It is he too to whom Jesus specially appears (Luke 24.34; 1 Cor. 15.5), after he has told him he would have to strengthen his brothers (Luke 22.32).

Thus the witness of the Gospels is sufficiently clear for the historian: Jesus chose a particular group of 'ministers', the Twelve, whose leader was Peter. This group of twelve was chosen to 'direct' the messianic people of Israel, and Jesus clearly prepared them for this responsibility even though the way he revealed his Messiahship and his glory utterly overthrew all the Twelve's former ideas.

The first chapters of Acts portray the community of Jerusalem in a very edifying fashion:

> And all who believed were together and had all things in common; and they sold their possessions and goods and distributed them to all, as any had need. And day by day, attending the temple together and breaking bread in their homes, they partook of food with glad and generous hearts, praising God and having favour with all the people. And the Lord added to their number day by day those who were being saved (Acts 2.44-7).

This somewhat idealized description must not mask the difficulties which the community had to face: persecutions from outside and, within, sanctions to be taken against certain hypocritical Christians (see Acts 5.1-11). One of the difficulties of community life was to find the solution to the problem of the ministry; twice, in Acts 1.15-26 and in 6.1-6, this was the central preoccupation of the first Christians.

The first passage recounts the election of Matthias in order to make up the group of the Twelve. If Jesus had chosen a company of twelve, it was because the figure *12* had a theological significance, as representing the twelve tribes of Israel. To speak of this group as 'the Twelve' sufficed to make the hearers understand that it stood for the leaders of the new Israel. Now 'one of the Twelve', Judas Iscariot, had committed suicide during Jesus's Passion (Matt. 27.3-5). The group is not whole and risks losing its significance in the eyes of other Jews. How is this to be dealt with?

Faced with such a situation, the Christians come together in a general assembly and meditate on the Scriptures. Their problem becomes clear in the light of Psalm 109.8, where it is written that when someone

7

is 'accursed', another must take his place. Peter then makes himself the spokesman for the Eleven and declares to the assembly:

So one of the men who have accompanied us during all the time that the Lord Jesus went in and out among us, beginning from the baptism of John until the day when he was taken up from us — one of these men must become with us a witness to his resurrection (Acts 1.21-2).

In order clearly to show that it is God who is choosing, they proceed by way of casting lots between two candidates. Matthias is chosen and numbered with the re-completed group of the Twelve. They can now truly take up their mission and bear witness to Jesus's resurrection (Acts 1.22; cf. 1Cor. 15.5) to 'the people of Israel' (Acts 2.22; 3.12; 5.35). This preaching by the Twelve, accompanied by miracles, gains a measure of success among the Jews of Jerusalem, a success which produces a new problem:

Now in these days when the disciples were increasing in number, the Hellenists murmured against the Hebrews because their widows were neglected in the daily distribution (Acts 6.1).

The tension which thus shows itself is easily explained. The Jews gathered in Jerusalem were of different origins. Some came originally from Palestine and their native tongue was Aramaic, written at this period in the same characters as Hebrew. Others came from the different Jewish communities of the Mediterranean basin, from the Diaspora, and their native language was Greek. These latter, the Hellenists, often belonged to less strict, more culturally 'open', backgrounds than the Palestinian Jews. Now the Twelve were all Hebrews born in Palestine. As they were responsible for the establishment of the community relief fund, they had the natural tendency to assist most those who spoke the same language as they, and the widows of the Hellenists were more or less neglected. To resolve this problem which threatened to tear the new-born Christian community apart, the Twelve call a general assembly of the disciples and propose a solution which goes to the heart of the problem. Since there are two different cultural groups, it is to be preferred that each group organizes itself as an autonomous community with its own ministers. So seven men from the Hellenists are chosen, the 'Seven', with Stephen as their leader, to take care of the ministry in the Hellenist community. The significance of the institution of the Seven, who have no connection with the 'deacons', cannot be overestimated: faced with a novel need in the Church, the Twelve do not hesitate to create a new ministerial framework and do not feel limited by the fact that Jesus only instituted the ministry of the Twelve.

Stephen, leader of the Seven, is a bold preacher who soon attracts to himself the hatred of the Hellenist Jews in Jerusalem. He is rapidly arrested, tried, and stoned (Acts 6–7), and a violent persecution is unleashed against the Christian community of the Hellenists, who are forced to scatter (Acts 8.1). From this point the group of the Seven has no more *raison d'etre* and disappears as a constituted body. Some of its members, like Philip (Acts 8.5-13), adapt themselves to the new situation and proclaim the good news elsewhere, in Samaria and in the towns of the Mediterranean coastline.

The Twelve soon suffer the same fate as the Seven. King Herod kills James the brother of John with the sword, and arrests Peter (Acts 12.2,3). Faced with so bloody a persecution, the survivors, Peter first, are forced to leave Jerusalem (Acts 12.17), and from this time there are no more references to the Twelve as a group. Such a rapid disappearance is astonishing. Why not have chosen a successor to James, as one was chosen to Judas? The persecution does not explain everything. In fact, at this time an important event marks a true turning-point in the life of the Christian community: the first pagans are admitted to the Church (Acts 10—11). The ministerial structure of the Twelve which had had special reference to the Israel of the twelve tribes has lost its *raison d'etre*; and, as with the setting-up of the Seven, the extension of the gospel to a new section of humanity will bring the creation of new forms of ministry.

The pagans are invited to call on the same God and to recognize the same Lord, as Israel does.

> But how are men to call upon him in whom they have not believed? And how are they to believe in him of whom they have never heard? And how are they to hear without a preacher? And how can men preach unless they are sent? (Rom. 10.14-15).

Paul thus sums up the motives which led to the organization of the missionary work of the 'apostles', a word which means 'one who is sent', a *missionary*. The epoch of great missionary work begins with the opening of the Church to the Gentiles, and will close with the deaths of the two great apostles, Peter and Paul, at Rome *c*. AD 64—7.

The organizing of this ministry of 'apostles' seems to appear for the first time in the important Christian community of Syrian Antioch. This was no accident. It was at Antioch that the Good News was for the first time preached to the Greeks (Acts 11.20), and there too 'the disciples were for the first time called Christians' (Acts 11.26). Acts tells us how this dynamic centre, led by ministers called 'prophets and teachers', decided by the inspiration of the Holy Spirit to send two of its members as missionaries, as 'apostles', to the island of Cyprus and the towns of southern Asia Minor (Acts 13.1-3). The names of these first two apostles have been preserved for us: Barnabas, and Saul who was later called Paul. The latter, who in Christian tradition is *the* apostle', was more precisely the apostle sent by the Antiochene community. So it is not surprising that when he lists in his letters the organization of the ministry in the Church, he names the ministers he knew at Antioch:

> God has appointed in the church
> first apostles,
> second prophets,
> third teachers . . . (1 Cor. 12.28).

We find this organization — apostles, prophets, teachers — in another missionary document of this period, also coming from the region of Antioch: the Didache (xi-xiii). Using its evidence, we can say with some precision what the role of each of these ministers was.

i The *apostles* are missionaries sent by an important Christian community to preach the Good News where it is as yet unknown. As soon as a Christian community is established firmly enough in any town, the apostle continues on his way in order to preach somewhere else. When his mission is over, he returns to the mother-community to give an account of his evangelistic work and its results (Acts 14.27; 18.22). So that they could better face the problems inherent in their mission, the apostles were normally sent out two by two: thus, Barnabas and Paul (Acts 13.2), Judas and Silas (Acts 15.27).

This missionary activity extended slowly over all the Mediterranean world. In order to avoid having two parties clashing in the same place, the leaders met together and set up a plan for apostolic work: the celebrated 'agreement of Jerusalem' mentioned by Paul in Galatians 2.9. The division of apostolic responsibility was not geographical but 'ethno-cultural'; there were apostles given the work of preaching to the Jews and others charged with announcing the Good News to the Gentiles. Each apostle was thus more or less a specialist, the two leading figures in the Mediterranean world being Paul 'an apostle to the Gentiles' (Rom. 11.13) and Peter, apostle to the Jews of the Dispersion (see 1 Pet. 1.1). This division by 'ethno-cultural' groupings explains how the two great apostles were to have preached the Good News in the same large towns — Antioch (Gal. 2.11), Rome (Acts 28.30), and perhaps Corinth (1 Cor. 1.12).

ii The *prophets* were recognized by their speaking 'in the Spirit' (Did. xi.7.8; 1 Cor. 14.29-32). Like the prophets of the Old Testament, their teaching could take the form of oracles, and Acts gives us two examples: the first one was proclaimed during the liturgical assembly of the Christian community of Antioch and is at the very foundation of the apostolate: 'Set apart for me Barnabas and Saul for the work to which I have called them' (Acts 13.2). The second was proclaimed in Caesarea by a prophet called Agabus; accompanying it with a symbolic gesture, he announced Paul's future imprisonment: *'Thus says the Holy*

Spirit, "So shall the Jews at Jerusalem bind the man who owns this girdle and deliver him into the hands of the Gentiles" ' (Acts 21.11).

The prophets generally played a prominent part in all assemblies for prayer. Entrusted with the proclamation of the Word of God, they gave what we today call the 'sermon', the 'homily', after the reading of Scripture; and led the thanksgiving, which we now call the 'eucharistic prayer' (Did. x.7; cf. 1 Cor. 14.15-17).

iii The *teachers* were almost always linked with the prophets, as the phrase 'prophets and teachers' shows (Acts 13.1; Did. xv.1). They gave more systematic instruction, based on Scripture, like the Jewish rabbis of that time. It is even probable that the majority of 'teachers' were converted rabbis; like Saul (Paul) who had studied the Jewish Law under the rabbi Gamaliel (Acts 22.3); or like Apollos, that 'eloquent man, well versed in the Scriptures', educated according to the exegetical traditions of the school of Alexandria (Acts 18.24).

The institution of these three specialized ministries, apostles, prophets, teachers, explains the extraordinary expansion of the Christian community of Antioch in the first century. All local churches, however, were not organized on this plan; the writings of the period give evidence of different kinds of ministry in other communities.

At Jerusalem, following the persecution of the Hellenists (Acts 6—7), the Christian community was essentially one of 'Hebrews'; they organized themselves along the traditional lines of Jewish communities, and put at their head a group of *presbyters* (= 'elders') presided over by James 'the Lord's brother'. These presbyters directed the community as much on the spiritual level — the study of the Law, moral and pastoral decisions (Acts 15) — as on the material level: oversight of the community's relief-funds (Acts 11.29 -30; Gal. 2.10). It was along the lines of this presbyteral organization that the Jewish-Christian communities of Cilicia and southern Asia Minor ordered themselves; the apostles, probably Judas and Silas (see Acts 15.22) 'appointed elders (*presbuteroi*). . . . in every church' (Acts 14.23).

Writing to the Thessalonians *c*. AD 50, the apostle Paul calls them to honour those who work hard for the community, and more precisely those who 'preside' and 'exhort' (see 1 Thess. 5.12-13).

Not far from Thessalonika, the church of Macedonian Philippi seems to have been led by 'overseers and ministers' (*episkopoi kai diakonoi*, Phil. 1.1); this double title probably refers to leaders of local Gentile-Christian communities dependent on the missionary centre of Antioch. For the Didache tells these communities:

> You must, then, elect for yourselves bishops and deacons [i.e., *overseers and ministers*] who are a credit to the Lord, men who are gentle, generous, faithful and well tried. For their ministry to you is identical with that of the prophets and teachers (Didache XV.1; E.T., *Library of Christian Classics*, vol. 1, ed. and tr. C. C. Richardson, 1953, p.178).

Thus in this period which we can call, in the precise meaning of the term, 'apostolic', the Church experienced a remarkable missionary expansion, willed and organized, and the Christian communities which came to birth in all sorts of places built themselves each on its own traditions.

By the time of the deaths of the two apostles, Peter and Paul, the Gospel had already reached the nerve-centres of the Mediterranean world: Rome, Corinth, Ephesus, Antioch, Caesarea, and probably Alexandria. The Christian communities in each of these great cities took care of the preaching of the Gospel in the surrounding towns and villages. After the period of geographical expansion came the time of consolidation. After the death of the eyewitnesses of the life and teaching of Jesus the leaders of the Church had particularly to ensure Christian fidelity to the Master's teaching and their unity in despite of geographical dispersion. It was the time of the 'evangelists and pastors' (Eph. 4.11).

The Christian authors of this period multiply their recommendations to the leaders of the local communities:

> Take heed to yourselves and to all the flock, in which the Holy Spirit has made you guardians (*episkopous*), to feed the church of the Lord (Acts 20.28).

> Tend the flock of God that is your charge, not by constraint but willingly, not for shameful gain but eagerly, not as domineering over those in your charge but being examples to the flock (1 Pet. 5.2-3).

These exhortations are often mingled with sharp warnings:

> I know that after my departure fierce wolves will come in among you, not sparing the flock; and from among your own selves will arise men speaking perverse things, to draw away the disciples after them. Therefore be alert . . . (Acts 20.29-31).

The polemical tone is rather astonishing; it indicates that the churches of this period have already experienced the pain of some pastors' unworthy conduct and of foolish discourses from certain preachers.

It was in this difficult ecclesial context that one of Paul's disciples wanted to remind everyone of certain definite rules, and he wrote the two letters to Timothy and the one to Titus which are called the Pastoral Epistles.

The author of these letters lays down first of all that Christian communities should organize themselves. 'This is why I left you in Crete, that you might amend what was defective and appoint elders (*presbyters*) in every town as I directed you' (Titus 1.5). The 'presbyters' set at the head of a community make its leadership sure and 'labour in preaching and teaching' (1 Tim. 5.17). These functions demand certain special aptitudes in the one who fulfils them: besides his moral qualities, the candidate 'manage his own household well' and be 'an apt teacher' (1 Tim. 3.4 & 2).

Alongside the presbyters, sometimes called *overseers* (*episkopoi*), the church of Ephesus also had *deacons*. They appear for the first time in 1 Timothy 3.8-13 in a paragraph which is not precise about their functions; we only know that the diaconate was exercised by men as well as women. There are however a few pointers to suggest that it was an itinerant ministry, under the leaders at the great Christian centres, who are called 'evangelists', like Timothy at Ephesus (2 Tim. 4.5), and Philip at Caesarea (Acts 21.8).

Whether pastors, presbyter-episkopoi, deacons or evangelists, at the close of the first century the Church's ministers seem especially concerned with leading the local churches; they watch over their unity and their fidelity to the Master's teaching.

The Pastoral Epistles conclude our swift historical sketch of the evolution of the ministry according to the evidence of the New Testament. The primitive Church knew several 'structures' for the ministry, and it is probably this diversity which strikes the historian. Even the Pastoral Epistles witness to organization and vocabulary still in evolution; the bishop does not stand out in them distinct from the presbyter. The three-fold hierarchy, absent from the New Testament, is clearly attested only from the letters of Ignatius of Antioch onwards.

This diversity and evolution pose a question for us: can we discover any abiding shape under the different forms of the Christian ministry in the New Testament? Are the Church's ministers different from those of other societies? These are the questions we wish to examine now by drawing out what is original in the ecclesial ministry.

New Testament principles of the Christian ministry

At the heart of the diversity of the ministry, the text of the New Testament permits us to see the fundamental characteristics which unite and make something new of Christian ministers.

The new Israel founded by Jesus is not, any more than the old Israel was, a faceless mass of men and women without bonds between them. Jesus himself was moved when he saw the crowds coming to him, and 'he had compassion on them, because they were like sheep without a shepherd' (Mark 6.34). In more precise words, when he spoke about the 'twelve thrones' (p. 5) Jesus showed very clearly that the messianic people must not only recognize its Head but also his 'ministers'. From the time of his mission in Galilee, the Twelve are summoned to share Jesus's pastoral responsibility, for he calls them to 'go . . . to the lost sheep of the house of Israel' (Matt.10.6).

Anarchy and disorder are never presented as a desirable lifestyle for God's people. Paul is particularly clear about this; reacting against the Corinthians' excesses he demands that their liturgical assemblies 'be done decently and in order' (1 Cor. 14.40), because 'God is not a God of confusion but of peace' (14.33). That is why he reminded the Thessalonians, addressing them in his first letter, that they must know how to appreciate and recognize his ministry (1 Thess. 5.12-13).

Two figures of speech express the vital necessity of order for the Church; the simile of the body (1 Cor. 12.12-30) and that of the house (3.10-15). These two we find fused in the letter to the Ephesians, where is described Christ's acts for his Church:

And his gifts were that some should be apostles, some prophets, some evangelists, some pastors and teachers, for the equipment of the saints, for the work of ministry, for building up the body of Christ, until we all attain to the unity of the faith and of the knowledge of the Son of God, to mature manhood, to the measure of the stature of the fullness of Christ; so that we may no longer be children, tossed to and fro and carried about with every wind of doctrine, by the cunning of men, by their craftiness in deceitful wiles. Rather, speaking the truth in love, we are to grow up in every way into him who is the head, into Christ, from whom the whole body, joined and knit together by every joint with which it is supplied, when each part is working properly, makes bodily growth and upbuilds itself in love (Eph. 4.11-16).

These exhortations and pictures are clear enough. According to the New Testament, the ideal of the Church is not to be simply a collection of individuals, each directly attached to the Christ: the Church must be an organized people, a structured community, for that is one of the concrete conditions for its life and growth.

The necessity of structures for the Church does not alter its true character at all; it is the Body of Christ, the people of God, the messianic community animated by the Holy Spirit (see Acts 2.17). The divine initiative is therefore at the root of the ministry as it is at the root of the Church. This is obvious already in the institution of the Twelve: at the moment of their being chosen, Mark underlines the initiative of Christ — he 'called to him those whom he desired' (Mark 3.13); and at Matthias's election they proceed by casting lots in order to emphasize that the ministry is given by God.

Luke and John in particular insist on the role of the Holy Spirit for the exercise of the ministry. It is 'by the Holy Spirit' that Jesus chose the Twelve (Acts 1.2) and it is the Holy Spirit who gave them power to witness 'to the end of the earth' (Acts 1.8). Such is the meaning of Pentecost: the manifestation of the gift of the Holy Spirit (Acts 2.4), which the Fourth Gospel places in direct dependence on Jesus: 'Receive the Holy Spirit. If you forgive the sins of any, they are forgiven; if you retain the sins of any, they are retained' (John 20.22-3).

No doubt there is some theological systematization by these two Evangelists, but this interpretation is nothing new. It is already the apostle Paul's, in his short treatise 'on spiritual gifts' in 1 Corinthians 12-14. For him, every ministry is a gift (*charisma*) made by the Holy Spirit to the Church, a gift even more important than that of speaking in tongues or working miracles. Why? because the ministry is far more useful in building up the congregation, for the growth of the Church. Thus we can understand the order of importance which Paul gives to the members of the Church in accordance with their gifts:

You are the Body of Christ and individually
  members of it.
And God has appointed in the church
first apostles,
second prophets,
third teachers,
then workers of miracles, then healers, helpers,
  administrators,
speakers in various kinds of tongues (1 Cor. 12.27-28).

These gifts are doubtless not the essential thing for the Christian life, for that is love — charity; yet it is quite natural to seek them, since they are useful in the Church: 'Make love your aim, and earnestly desire the spiritual gifts, especially that you may prophesy' (1 Cor. 14.1).

We see here how any opposition between 'charismatic' and 'institutional' ministry is strange to Paul's thought. As far as he is concerned, every ministry is a gift of the Holy Spirit to the Church.

Like the prophets of the Old Testament filled with the Spirit of Yahweh, the ministers of the New Covenant act under the inspiration of the Holy Spirit, and especially when preaching the Good News. St Luke is emphatic about this: The Twelve (Acts 2.4), Peter

(4.8), the Seven (6.3), Stephen (6.5,10; 7.55), Philip (8.29,39), Saul (9.17), the apostles Barnabas and Paul (13.4,9) act and speak 'full of the Holy Spirit'; and we find the same theology again in the Pastoral Epistles:

> Hence I remind you to rekindle the gift of God that is within you through the laying on of my hands; for God did not give us a spirit of timidity but a spirit of power and love and self-control.
>
> Do not be ashamed then of testifying to our Lord, nor of me his prisoner, but take your share of suffering for the gospel in the power of God (2 Tim. 1.6-8).

The minister in the Church is then 'the man of the Spirit'.

The fact that the ministry is a gift of the Holy Spirit explains the importance given to the authority of the minister in the Church. By a contrast with purely human societies where the chief often appears merely to be the representative of the majority of members in the group: in the Church the authority of the minister, whatever the means by which he is chosen, is not a straightforward delegation of power from the Christian body. His authority represents the authority of Christ. True, only Christ is 'the head of the body, the Church' (Col. 1.18) and all other authority can only be dependent on his, delegated by him, exercised by his Name.

Yet at the moment of their first ministry in Galilee, Jesus gives the Twelve 'authority over the unclean spirits' (Mark 6.7), and on their return they tell him, 'Master, even the demons are subject to us in your name!' (Luke 10.17). Christ's ministers are then his representatives, his *chargés d'affaires*; to welcome them is to welcome Christ (Matt. 10.40) and their

21

decisions are ratified by Christ himself:

> Truly, I say to you, whatever you bind on earth
> shall be bound in heaven, and whatever you loose
> on earth shall be loosed in heaven (Matt. 18.18;
> cf. 16.18).

This is true not just for the Twelve but for every
minister. St Paul repeats it frequently: his authority
comes from Christ, it is the authority of Christ.

> For even if I boast a little too much of our author-
> ity, which the Lord gave for building you up and
> not for destroying you, I shall not be put to shame
> (2 Cor. 10.8; cf. 13.10).

> Jesus Christ our Lord, through whom we have
> received grace and apostleship to bring about the
> obedience of the faith for the sake of his name
> among all the nations (Rom. 1.50).

Generally, when the apostle exhorts his readers, he
does it in the Name of the Lord:

> . . . we beseech and exhort you *in the Lord Jesus*
> . . . you know what instructions we gave you
> *through the Lord Jesus* (1 Thess. 4. 1-2).

> Such persons we command and exhort *in the Lord
> Jesus Christ* to do their work in quietness and to
> earn their own living (2 Thess. 3.12).

Exhortation can become threatening:

> If anyone refuses to obey we say in this letter,
> note that man, and have nothing to do with him,
> that he may be ashamed (2 Thess. 3.14).

The threat can even end in sanctions, as the excommu-
nication of the incestuous brother of Corinth shows:

Though absent in body I am present in spirit, and as if present, I have already pronounced judgement *in the name of the Lord Jesus* on the man who has done such a thing. When you are assembled, and my spirit is present, *with the power of our Lord Jesus*, you are to deliver this man to Satan for the destruction of the flesh, that his spirit may be saved in the day of the Lord Jesus (1 Cor. 5.3-5).

When we come to see the reality of the ministerial authority it should make us tremble with fear and wonder before 'such power given to men' (Matt. 9.8). Indeed, there is great temptation to make demi-gods of them (Acts 10.25-6; 14.11-15). Nothing could be more opposed to the gospel.

After being chosen by Jesus, the Twelve — who did not lack ambition — started to argue which of them would be the greatest, who would have the first place (Mark 9.34-5; 10.35-40). It is against this background that Jesus explains what must be the attitude of those ministers whom he has chosen:

You know that those who are supposed to rule over the Gentiles lord it over them, and their great men exercise authority over them. But it shall not be so among you; but whoever would be great among you must be your *servant*, and whoever would be first among you must be slave of all. For the Son of man also came not to be served but *to serve*, and to give his life as a ransom for many (Mark 10.42-5).

The Minister's behaviour must be identical with the Messiah's. After the symbolic act of the foot-washing, Jesus emphasized the abiding meaning of that example:

23

When he had washed their feet, and taken his garments, and resumed his place, he said to them, 'Do you know what I have done to you? You call me Teacher and Lord; and you are right, for so I am. If I then, your Lord and Teacher, have washed your feet, you also ought to wash one another's feet. For I have given you an example, that you also should do as I have done to you' (John 13.12-15).

It is hard to put things more clearly: Jesus obviously realized that he was putting forward something new and original, which went against all the usual ways of exercising human responsibility. The Twelve were no more than anyone else ready to adopt such an attitude, and that explains why Jesus insists on this important facet of the ministry.

Paul tried to carry out in his life this complete attitude of service; thus:

What then is Apollos? What is Paul? Servants. . . (1 Cor. 3.5).

This is how one should regard us, as servants of Christ and stewards of the mysteries of God (1 Cor. 4.1).

For though I am free from all men, I have made myself a slave to all. . . (1 Cor. 9.19).

In this spirit he insists on not being a burden to the community (see 1 Thess. 2.5-7, 9; 2 Cor. 12, 13) and when he feels obliged to re-affirm his authority, he then stresses its ultimate purpose; to serve the growth of the Christians and the building-up of the Church (2 Cor. 10.8; cf. 13.10).

This fashion of using authority is rediscovered in the first letter of Peter as being of value:

> Tend the flock of God that is your charge, not by constraint but willingly, not for shameful gain but eagerly, not as domineering over those in your charge but being examples to the flock (1 Pet. 5.2-3).

as well as in the Pastoral Epistles, where Timothy, the 'evangelist', is called on to be a 'good servant of Christ Jesus' (1 Tim. 4.6).

The author of the third letter of John feels himself compelled to denounce 'Diotrephes, who likes to put himself first' in the Church (v.9). This demonstrates very well how far the gospel principle is unnatural for men; the Church's ministers will always find it hard to live up to it.

The Fourth Gospel strongly affirms that the service of the Word of God is the proper end of Christ's mission and authority:

> You say that I am a king. For this I was born, and for this I have come into the world, to bear witness to the truth (John 18.37; cf. Mark 1.38).

This service is the first task of the Twelve, from the moment of their first mission in Galilee:

> Preach as you go, saying, 'The kingdom of heaven is at hand' (Matt. 10.7).

This priority given to the Word is even more clearly affirmed in Acts and in Paul's letters.

After Matthias's election the ministry of the Twelve consists essentially in witnessing in Israel to the resurrection (Acts 1.15-26); which is why, a little later, Peter and John retort to the Sanhedrin's threats:

> Whether it is right in the sight of God to listen to

you rather than to God, you must judge; for we cannot but speak of what we have seen and heard (Acts 4.19-20).

Even more clearly, when the oversight of the common fund looks like taking up too much time and when a choice must be made, the Twelve openly declare:

It is not right that we should give up preaching the word of God to serve tables (Acts 6.2).

As for Paul's views, we have only to recall the well-known sentence, 'Christ did not send me to baptize but to preach the gospel' (1 Cor. 1.17); it obviously means that the preaching of the Word is the first task of an apostle.

This priority is also found in the Pastoral Epistles, where the most important presbyters are 'those who labour in preaching and teaching' (1 Tim. 5.17). So it is not surprising that a candidate for office must be 'an apt teacher' (1 Tim. 3.2; cf. Titus 1.9). It is in the same spirit that the writer makes the following recommendations to Timothy:

Attend to the public reading of scripture, to preaching, to teaching (1 Tim. 4.13).

Preach the word, be urgent in season and out of season, convince, rebuke, and exhort, be unfailing in patience and in teaching (2 Tim. 4.2).

According, then, to the New Testament the first concrete task of the minister is to carry on the proclamation of the Good News brought by Christ.

Several texts of the New Testament seem to carry even further this priority given to the gospel in the work of the Church's ministry. If the authorities must be at the service of the Word of God, it means that one must choose obedience to the gospel over obedience to ministers, if these latter are no longer faithful to the gospel.

The authentic letters of Paul offer two pieces of evidence on these lines. The first is an historical scene: at Antioch Paul opposed Peter and Barnabas because 'they were not straightforward about the truth of the gospel' (Gal. 2.14). The second is in a hypothesis which Paul puts into his letter to the Galatians:

> If we, or an angel from heaven, should preach to you a gospel contrary to that which we preached to you, let him be accursed. As we have said before, so now I say again, if anyone is preaching to you a gospel contrary to that which you received, let him be accursed (Gal. 1.8-9).

This solemn declaration demonstrates well the limits of the minister's authority. It comes from Christ and only exists if it is in accord with the Lord's will. Where there is unfaithfulness to the gospel, Paul recognizes the existence of a duty of disobedience to those who have authority in the Church.

In questions of authority within the community, Jesus is our pattern:

> I am the good shepherd;
> I know my own and my own know me, . . .
> And I lay down my life for the sheep.
> I have other sheep, that are not of this fold;
> I must bring them also
> And they will heed my voice.
> So there shall be one flock, one shepherd
> (John 10.14-16).

The Twelve share with Christ the responsibility of

gathering in the new Israel (cf. the saying about the 'twelve thrones', Matt. 19.28: see also p. 5). This is implicit already in the first mission in Galilee, for Jesus tells them, 'Go. . . to the lost sheep of the house of Israel' (Matt. 10.6). It is a very hard calling. Jesus, in opposition to the usual ideas of his day, demands that the poor and the weak should have their place in this new Israel, while the Twelve have the inclination to rebuff them:

> They were bringing children to him, that he might touch them; and the disciples rebuked them. But when Jesus saw it, he was indignant, and said to them, 'Let the children come to me, do not hinder them; for to such belongs the kingdom of God' (Mark 10.13-14).

> Whoever receives one such child in my name receives me; and whoever receives me, receives not me but him who sent me (Mark 9.37).

The Twelve must therefore undertake their responsibilities in a completely new way, and Jesus insists on a special manner of showing authority among the people of the Messiah.

> But you are not to be called rabbi for you have one teacher, and you are all brethren. And call no man your father on earth, for you have one Father, who is in heaven. Neither be called masters, for you have one master, the Christ. He who is greatest among you shall be your servant (Matt. 23.8-11).

Among God's people the exercise of authority must always preserve a brotherly relationship. This original thinking is highlighted in the Pastoral Epistles. The writer recommends Timothy to have simple and natural relationships with all the members of the community:

Do not rebuke an older man
but exhort him as you would a father;
treat younger men like brothers, older women like
mothers,
younger women like sisters, in all purity.

(1 Tim. 5.1-2).

Thus Timothy is not to put himself above the community, or as its 'father'; in carrying out his mission he must take a natural place in relation to the different members of the community where a completely family atmosphere is paramount.

This principle demonstrates again the original way in which authority is exercised in the new Israel, and here too, of course, Jesus runs counter to the spontaneous ideas of the Twelve. Since Jesus had sent them officially with power to act in his Name (Mark 6.7-8), they naturally imagined that this power was reserved to them; they wanted to eliminate 'illegitimate' competitors. It all happens when the Twelve return from their mission. John says to Jesus, 'Teacher, we saw a man casting out demons in your name, and we forbade him, because he was not following us'. But Jesus says to him, 'Do not forbid him; for no one who does a mighty work in my name will be able soon after to speak evil of me' (Mark 9.38-9). Jesus's reply is perfectly clear. Not even the Twelve, officially sent out by him, can claim a monopoly of official action in his Name; they are only 'unworthy servants' (Luke 17.10), and the Master remains free to act by other intermediaries.

The same principle of the absence of all monopoly occurs again in St Paul, when he reflects on the spiritual gifts in the Church (1 Cor. 12-14). If for him the charismata of the apostles, prophets and teachers are the most important, they do not exhaust the manifold nature of God's gifts to his Church: 'then [there are] workers of miracles, then healers, helpers, administrators, speakers in various kinds of tongues' (1 Cor. 12.28). Speaking generally, indeed, 'each has his own special gift from God, one of one kind and one of another' (1 Cor. 7.7). So we find 'As each has received a gift, employ it for one another, as good stewards of God's varied grace' (1 Pet. 4.10).

Not only may authority make no claim to any monopoly, but also it must be exercised in close association with the community. Thus, as regards the first gospel, the power of binding and loosing is not given solely to Cephas (Matt. 16.19) but to all the ministers and to the whole community (Matt. 18.17-18). Paul himself is bent on making the whole community share in his decision to excommunicate the incestuous member at Corinth: 'When *you are assembled, and my spirit is present*. . .' (1 Cor. 5.4). This vital role of the general assembly of Christians at moments of crisis is attested from the foundation of the Church, in particular in resolving the tensions between Hellenists and Hebrews (Acts 6.2-5).

These few examples serve clearly to show that the exercise of authority in the Church is unable to do without active participation by the community: the minister cannot claim for himself a monopoly of all gifts and services which the community needs in order to develop.

At the end of this summing-up of the fundamental characteristics of the ecclesial ministry in the New Testament, we can see more clearly its greatness and its bounds. Its greatness is there because it represents the authority of Christ, head of his Church, and therefore it plays a prominent part in the life and growth of the people of God. Its bounds are set by the understanding that the ministry is only a way of service whose importance is limited by ends assigned: the proclamation of the Word of God, the leading of the Christian community in accordance with the gospel.

Some concrete aspects of ministerial life

Having sorted out the fundamental and original orientations of the Christian ministry, let us quickly call to mind the New Testament witness on some particular aspects of ministerial life. Each of the points to be tackled would merit, in itself, a detailed study; we shall only be able to offer general conclusions. We shall call to mind the choosing of ministers, the problem of their ordination and of their role in the eucharist, the ministry of women, the family ties of ministers, their remuneration, and the problem of the continuity of the ministry.

We have seen that it was Jesus himself who chose the Twelve, and that at the time of the election of Matthias, suitable characteristics were decided upon, after which two candidates were chosen (Acts 1.21-2); the final decision was then taken by casting lots, thus underlining that it was God who gave this ministry to men.

This method of proceeding by lot seems to have been an exception. When the Seven were called, things happened more simply. It began with a statement of the characteristics needed for this ministry, characteristics put forward by the Twelve and accepted by the assembly. The assembly then chose from its own number the seven future ministers who had the necessary qualifications.

31

When Paul wanted to associate with himself a secretary-assistant to help him in his mission, it was on the express recommendation of 'the brethren at Lystra and Iconium' (Acts 16.2) that he chose Timothy; the community from which he set out was thus closely associated with the choosing of an itinerant minister.

Paul acted differently in his relations with the Corinthian community. The lack of a true ministry in that church probably explains the failure to react to specific disorders there: and that is why the apostle himself takes the initiative in presenting a candidate who appeared able to take up the ministry to this turbulent community:

> You know that the household of Stephanas were the first converts in Achaia, and they have devoted themselves to the service of the saints; I urge you to be subject to such men and to every fellow worker and labourer (1 Cor. 16.15-16).

It is important to emphasize that even in this case Paul does not act in an authoritative way; he does not impose, but proposes with a warm testimonial. The Corinthians are still free to accept or reject the candidate.

In other churches the community's role is even more marked. It was the Philippians who had chosen Epaphroditus (Phil. 2.25), and probably the Colossians who marked out Epaphras (Col. 4.12). Paul simply recognizes their choice when he remarks on the value of these two ministers.

Several communities of Asia Minor followed the Jewish customs. According to Acts 14.23 and Titus 1.5, the presbyters of these communities, probably elected or co-opted by the members, were installed by apostles or 'evangelists' whose work was to visit a whole region.

Thus the procedure for choosing ministers varied with the communities. We can only draw the general conclusion that this choice seems to have been the result of an agreement between the general assembly of Christians and the ministers who were already exercising their office.

We must here emphasize the fragmentary nature of our sources concerning ordination, which give us only indirect information about the liturgy of the first Christian community.

Two reports, that of the institution of the Seven (Acts 6.6) and that of the sending out of the first 'apostles' (Acts 13.3), refer to a ceremony of institution which included the laying-on of hands; but the text does not clearly indicate who laid on hands in either case.

The evidence of the Pastoral Epistles is more definite: there we find several references to an ordination of Timothy by Paul:

> Do not neglect the gift (*charisma*) you have, which was given you by prophetic utterance when the elders laid their hands upon you (1 Tim. 4.14).

> Hence I remind you to rekindle the gift (*charisma*) of God that is within you through the laying on of my hands (2 Tim 1.6; cf. 1 Tim. 1.18; 6.12).

This ceremony comprised a profession of faith on the part of the candidate (1 Tim. 6.12; cf. 1 Tim. 1.18); a prophecy, that is to say an official liturgical prayer said over the candidate (1 Tim. 1.18); and a laying-on of hands (see 1 Tim. 5.22). The Greek phrase used to speak of this laying-on of hands

33

corresponds to a Hebrew expression which, in Jewish tradition, refers to the ordination of a rabbi. In accordance with the whole context of the Pastoral Epistles that would mean that this 'ordination' of Timothy essentially guaranteed, in the eyes of the community, the teaching given by one so ordained.

In the absence of other witnesses it appears very hazardous to affirm that ordination with the laying-on of hands was the usual ceremony by which ministers were invested. Ordination only appears clearly attested for presbyters, in fact, where churches of the Jewish tradition had adopted as a model the rabbinic ordination, whose archetype is found in the Old Testament (Deut. 34.9). We have no evidence for the Gentile-Christian churches which were not led by presbyters.

A glance at a concordance of the vocabulary of the New Testament reveals that the word 'priest' is never used in a sacerdotal meaning (Gk = *hiereus*) in speaking of the ministers of the Church. Yet ministerial activity was not alien to the eucharistic assembly. On the contrary, in Acts 20.7-11, Luke describes a 'Sunday' worship-meeting of the first Christians. Now Paul is the central figure of the two principal activities of this meeting. He it is who teaches and who 'breaks the bread', a clear enough reference to the eucharistic meal. This double activity exactly corresponds to the two fundamental tasks of the minister; servant of the Word (teaching) and of the community (presiding at the eucharistic meal). The apostle therefore was playing a role in the foreground in the liturgical assemblies. The assumptions of the first letter to the Corinthians and of the Didache about the activities of the prophets (*supra*) confirm the importance of the role

34

of these ministers in the liturgical assembly. These 'prophets' not only took care of the preaching, the exhortation addressed to the community, but they also spoke the eucharistic prayer.

Generally speaking, the numerous references relating to the presidential functions of the ministers, in particular those of the presbyters (e.g., 1 Tim. 5.17) probably relate to their special place in the assemblies for worship, and in conformity with the Jewish tradition are consistent with their role of presiding and invoking the blessing at the eucharistic meal.

Women had no official place, in Jewish tradition, either in the synagogue worship or in political life. Yet several women had played special parts in Jesus's Galilean ministry (Luke 8.2-3), although in a discreet fashion; and he did not hesitate to enter into conversation with a woman, to the surprise of his disciples (John 4.27). So it is not astonishing to find in Acts that women take important parts in certain Christian communities, especially those of the Hellenists and those made up of Gentiles. Thus the four daughters of the evangelist Philip used to prophesy at Caesarea (Acts 21.9), while Lydia is shown to be very active at Philippi; and at Ephesus, before the arrival of Paul there, Priscilla and Aquila appear to have taken on together the task of directing the community (see Acts 18.26-7).

The Pauline letters supply us with very valuable direct evidence on this problem, evidence which seems at first sight contradictory. In fact, if we omit 1 Corinthians 14.34-5, where literary critics recognize an interpolation from 1 Timothy 2.11-14, Paul appears to accept the ministry of women as a normal thing. He specifically recognizes, in precise terms, in

1 Corinthians 11.2-16, that women may 'pray' and 'prophesy' (11.5), that is to say that they can take on the most important ministry in a local church, the ministry of the 'prophet' (see p.13). This principle is confirmed by several express allusions; thus in Romans 16.1-2, Paul emphatically recommends Phoebe as 'a minister (the word *diakonos* had not yet its technical meaning of 'deacon') of the church at Cenchreae'. Further, the personal greetings of Romans 16, Colossians 4.15, and Philemon vv.1,2 demonstrate the important place which women, often with their husbands, occupied in the early Church. The admission of women to the ministry is, besides, fully in accordance with the apostle's idea of the Church:

> There is neither Jew nor Greek
> slave nor free
> male nor female;
> for you are all one in Christ Jesus (Gal. 3.28).

Yet the ministry of women does not appear to have been accepted without restriction in every church. On the contrary, in the Pastoral Epistles, the author (markedly in the Jewish tradition) bluntly forbids women to teach and thus to exercise the presbyteral ministry:

> Let a woman learn in silence, with all submissiveness. I permit no woman to teach. . . (1 Tim. 2.11-12).

He appears, indeed to limit women to the diaconal ministry (1 Tim. 3.11) because the latter probably did not include the official duty of teaching.

We may say that the exercise of ecclesial ministry by women did not seem to pose any doctrinal problem; St Paul's reflections on the Church clearly allowed the possibility, but the problem lay in the pastoral adaptation of the principle to the differing cultural background of each community.

In the New Testament the ministry is exercised equally by married people like Peter, and by the unmarried, bachelors or widowers, like Paul. Except for the apostles Paul and Barnabas (see 1 Cor. 9.5-6) and the daughters of the evangelist Philip (Acts 21.9), the ministers of the early Church generally seem to have been married. What we have just seen in examining the role of couples who led and directed the Pauline communities is confirmation of this. But it is the Pastoral Epistles, against the background of Jewish tradition, which are most explicit on this point. The writer emphasizes that a candidate for the ministry should be 'a faithful husband' (*lit.* 'the husband of one wife', 1 Tim. 3.2, 12; Titus 1.6), and a good father of his family, concerned deeply for the upbringing of his children (1 Tim. 3. 4-5, 12; Titus 1.6).

So while recognizing the value of the charisma of celibacy for some ministers (1 Cor. 7.7-8), we can see clearly that the ministers of the early Church were usually married people.

When we come to ministers' remuneration, we have to distinguish between principle and practice. The principle is set out clearly by Paul, who leans upon the gospel tradition: 'The Lord commanded that those who proclaim the gospel should get their living by the gospel' (1 Cor. 9.14); 'the labourer deserves his wages' (Luke 10.7; cf. Matt. 10.10; 1 Tim. 5.18).

As we see, this principle is one of the best-attested of the New Testament. Since the itinerant minister had consecrated his life to the proclamation of the Good News, it was natural that the Christian community should take care of the material needs of the minister and his wife, if she accompanied him (1 Cor. 9.4-5; cf. 2 Cor. 11.8).

This principle, however, did not automatically affect the ministers in the local churches, and it seems that as far as they were concerned, the corresponding responsibility of the community was less than total. The proof-texts for this point:

> Let him who is taught the word share all good things with him who teaches (Gal. 6.6).

> Let the elders who rule well be considered worthy of double honours, especially those who labour in preaching and teaching (1 Tim. 5.17).

If they imply some payment, they do not necessarily mean that there is complete responsibility for all income. What is said in 1 Timothy 5.17 suggests that the payment was more or less, according to the time spent in ministering. Those who were concerned with a teaching ministry would have to devote the greater part of their time to it, while other ministers could continue to live by their trade.

Paul's own example, in any case, shows that the minister might refuse the community's contributions, when he judged it pastorally useful, and work with his own hands to provide for his needs (see 1 Thess. 2.9; 2 Thess. 3.7-9; 1 Cor. 9.1-18, etc.). In such circumstances the minister would again take up the trade he had followed before being called to the ministry.

To sum up, it would appear that the problem of the remuneration of the minister was solved by taking into account the wide range of every concrete situation.

At the very beginning of the Church's history, she was faced with the problem of the continuity of the ministry, by the mere fact of the disappearance of a minister. It was the death of Judas that led the first community of Jerusalem to choose a successor to him by appointing Matthias (Acts 1.15-26). This decision, taken after meditating on Scripture, clearly shows that the ministry must be continued, whatever the hazards of the ministers' lives. One of the concerns of the leaders of the Church will thus be to ensure the continuity of the ministry in a proper way.

The problem of the continuity or permanence of the ministry presented itself, indeed, on two clearcut occasions; when an itinerant minister moved on, and when the leader of a local church was no longer available.

In so far as the itinerant minister, apostle or even prophet or teacher was residing among the new, growing Christian community, or was visiting it regularly, it was he who in the first place provided ministry in that community. Although he might settle permanently in the community (Did. xiii), generally speaking he would have to leave it one day and go to preach the gospel elsewhere. The community then might find itself without a ministry, and so dwindle. To avoid this happening, the local church had to choose from its own members ministers for itself:

> You must, then, elect for yourselves bishops and deacons who are a credit to the Lord, men who are gentle, generous, faithful and well tried. For their ministry to you is identical with that of the prophets and teachers. You must not, therefore, despise them, for along with the prophets and teachers they enjoy a place of honour among you (Didache XV.1—2; E.T., *Library of Christian Classics*, vol. 1, ed. and tr. C. C. Richardson, 1953, p. 178).

St Paul applied the same principles when he

recommended in his letters to the new communities that they should learn how to treat their new ministers properly (see p.38), while in the Jewish-Christian churches the authenticity of these new ministers was guaranteed by their ordination by apostles sent from Jerusalem (Acts 14.23).

After the deaths of the great apostles, the problem of the continuity and authenticity of the ministry is the central concern of the writer of the Pastoral Epistles. Timothy and Titus must not just be contented to be faithful in teaching and to have the spirit of service in exercising their authority; they must also take care to ensure the handing-on of the gospel which the Apostle preached. After his death, they must both keep this gospel intact, not letting it be watered-down. This is already partly the role of the presbyters ordained by Timothy (1 Tim. 5.22) or Titus (Titus 1.5). However, this does not yet seem enough to this disciple of St Paul; he is emphatic in putting down clearly his point of view on the subject:

> What you have heard from me before many witnesses entrust to faithful men who will be able to teach others also (2 Tim. 2.2).

Timothy must therefore take steps to see that whatever may be the fate of the individual ministers, the 'word of God is not fettered' (2 Tim. 2.9) which means that he must groom a capable successor to continue the faithful proclamation of the gospel. That, no doubt, is how we are to understand the fine sentence put into Paul's mouth:

> I know whom I have believed and I am sure that he is able to guard until that Day what has been entrusted to me = ['my gospel', 2 Tim. 2.8] (2 Tim. 1.12).

40

Faithful transmission of the gospel will thus be assured until the close of the age (see Matt. 28.20).

The results of the investigation we have just made into the text of the New Testament will be very useful in throwing light on contemporary Christian thinking about the ministry. It now seems possible that we can draw some important conclusions.

The historical study has shown us, first, that the structure of the ministry evolved, that it differed according to the local churches and the time. It would then be natural that it should continue to evolve, in order to adapt itself to each church and each period. The New Testament has not canonized any one structure of ministry.

If, however, no hard and fast rule is made regarding any ministerial structure in the Church, certain general principles concerning the meaning and the exercise of these ministries are quite clearly affirmed in the New Testament. The second part of our investigation has allowed us to distinguish some of these fundamental ideas: the ministry shapes the Church, the authority of the minister represents Christ's authority; authority must be thought of as a means of service — more precisely, a service of the Word and of the community, respecting the 'charisms' of the other members of God's people.

The third section has shown us that the early Church had solved the main concrete problem concerning the way of life of its ministers by showing itself supple and resourceful in adapting to different situations. The study of later history will allow us to see to what degree the Church has continued to demonstrate the same pastoral judgement, in faithfulness to the principles of the gospel.

2

THE HISTORY OF THE CHURCH

Nearly twenty centuries separate us from the coming of Christ and the birth of the Church. During this time the Church has tried, sometimes well, sometimes badly, to live in that eternal life offered by Christ, in faithful response to the gospel summons, in the midst of the events and upheavals of world history in which her leaders have sometimes taken a very direct part. All this past history has affected, positively and negatively, our present understanding of the Church's ministry. Before we reflect on the fundamental meaning and the differing forms of ministry in today's Church, it is indispensable for us to recall the principal events of the history which still controls our lives; they will help us to understand better what is involved in the manifold questions being asked at the present time.

In the course of these twenty centuries the Church has known diverse forms of ministry and has tried to give each a theological interpretation. In presenting here the important stages of this history we shall try to understand better these two aspects of the Church's life — what is lived, and its interpretation. That is to say the story must be both the history of institutions and men, and the history of ideas.

In addition to the canonical collection of the New Testament texts, tradition has preserved for us several Christian writings dating from the end of the first century and, more especially, from the beginning of the second. We generally call them the writings of the

Apostolic Fathers. As well as the Didache originating from Antioch, this collection includes writings from Rome (*the Letter of Clement of Rome to the Corinthians* and *the Shepherd of Hermas*) and others originating from Asia Minor (*the Letters of Ignatius of Antioch* and *the Letter of Polycarp of Smyrna*).

It was a crisis in the ministerial organization of the church of Corinth which was the cause of Clement of Rome's letter: certain members of the Corinthian community had rebelled against their presbyters. In this conflict, Rome upheld the authority of the ministers; since the latter had committed no crime, there was no reason to deprive them of their office. The rebels must submit or leave the community. In putting forward this solution, Clement of Rome probably had at the back of his mind the analogy from the practice of Jewish communities in which 'elders' or 'presbyters' held their office for life unless they committed a grave fault.

This last-mentioned possibility was not a mere theory. Polycarp, in his letter to Philippi, approved the deposition of the presbyter Valens, for he had been guilty of a grave fault, with his wife as accomplice (to judge from Polycarp's sharp denunciation of avarice, Valens and his wife were probably guilty of misappropriating funds from the coffers of the community). On this occasion, Polycarp asks the presbyters of Philippi to demonstrate their zeal and kindness in carrying out their pastoral duties, without making any reference to the ministry of the word.

The witness of the Shepherd of Hermas is often hard to understand properly, on account of its special literary genre and the composite nature of its editing. It permits us, none the less, to glimpse the ministerial organization of the Church that it knew: presbyters are at the head of the church, they preside over it

(*Vis.* ii 4.3) and in concrete terms, they occupy the principal seats at the assemblies (*Vis.* iii 9.7). The ministry of the word, hardly mentioned in connection with the presbyters, seems above all to be the concern of the 'prophets', of whom Hermas is the type (*Mand.* xii 3.3): 'the prophesying angel who is close to him fills this man, and he filled with the Holy Spirit speaks to the crowd as the Lord wills' (*Mand.* xi 9). Presbyter and prophet together complete the ministry of the local church; the first exercises authority, the other attends to the ministry of the word — but only under the presbyter (*Mand.* xi 8.2).

The problems of the exercise of authority in the Christian community and of the organization of the ministry are at the heart of the letters of Ignatius of Antioch. He insists that all Christians must obey one leader, *the bishop*:

> Nobody must do anything that has to do with the church without the bishop's approval. You should regard that eucharist as valid which is celebrated by the bishop or by someone he authorizes... But he who acts without the bishop's knowledge is in the devil's service (Ignatius of Antioch. *ad. Smyrn.* 8.1; 9.1; E.T., *Library of Christian Classics*, vol. 1, ed. and tr. C. C. Richardson, 1953, p. 115).

Nothing could be clearer in speaking of the authority of the bishop, who is responsible for the whole Church. But he does not bear his burden alone: 'Follow the bishop, as Jesus Christ followed the Father, and the presbyters as the apostles; as for the deacons, respect them as you do the Law of God' (*ad. Smyrn.* 8.1). Thus the bishop must find support in the council of presbyters of the community, the *presbyterium*, for the unity of the community depends on the harmony existing between the bishop and his presbyterium; and its members must be in accord with the bishop 'like the strings of a lute' (*ad Eph*. 4.1).

The *deacons* who are mentioned in the letter of Polycarp as well as in the letters of Ignatius, seem to serve the bishop directly. They can undertake missionary journeys, keep in touch with other churches, and share in the ministry of the 'word of God' (*ad Phil*. 11.1).

In agreement with the indications of the Pastoral Epistles, the diaconate could also be exercised by women. We have exceptional evidence for this from a Roman magistrate, Pliny the Younger, writing from Bithynia in AD 112 about the legal problems posed by the persecution of Christians: the results of a 'police' investigation of two deaconesses deserves his mention in the report:

They declared that the sum of their guilt or error had amounted only to this, that on an appointed day they had been accustomed to meet before daybreak, and to sing a hymn antiphonally to Christ, as to a god, and to bind themselves by an oath [*sacramentum*] not for the commission of any crime, but to abstain from theft, robbery adultery, and breach of faith, and not to deny a deposit when it was claimed. After the conclusion of this ceremony it was their custom to depart but to meet again to take food; but it was ordinary and harmless food; and they had ceased this practice after my edict in which, in accordance with your orders, I had forbidden secret societies. I thought it the more necessary, therefore, to find out what truth there was in this by applying torture to two maidservants, who were called deaconesses [*ministrae*] but I found nothing except a depraved and extravagant superstition (Bk x, letter 96.7–8; E.T., *Documents of the Christian Church*, selected and edited by Henry Bettenson, 2nd edn., 1967, pp. 3–4).

This official evidence reminds us of the historical situation in which Christians lived during the time of the Apostolic Fathers. Their lives were often threatened by persecution, which, as always, struck at their leaders. Indeed, Ignatius of Antioch and Polycarp died as martyrs; one at Rome and the other at Smyrna. This background of persecution explains why the leaders of the Church harp so constantly on the theme of unity during this period. Faced with persecution they must 'form square' round the leaders who know they are risking their lives.

The historical background explains too the attempts to organize the ministry which mark this period of the apostolic fathers. We are watching the gradual spread of the three-fold ministry until it becomes the norm. The presbyteral pattern nearly managed to do it, but it was changed; it was completed by bringing forward one of the members of the presbyterium who became the leader and the representative of the local church — the bishop; while the other ministers, the prophets or deacons, played a more subdued part. The prophets were soon to disappear, while the deacons as the bishop's assistants would reinforce his authority and the efficiency of the episcopate. The three-fold hierarchy — bishops, presbyters, deacons — which first appeared at Antioch and in Asia Minor, is going to extend itself little by little throughout the second century to every local church. This growth in uniformity of the ministerial structure in the Church is accompanied by a greater emphasis on pastoral authority; somewhat to the detriment of the ministry of the Word, it seems.

It was in the second and third centuries that the Christian Church took the sociological shape which it has kept in all essentials down to our own days in the Catholic and Orthodox communions (P. Nautin, *Revue de droit canonique*, xxiii (1973), p. 47).

In spite of an outward calm, this period was marked by an important evolution in ministerial organization and by a no less important evolution in the concept of the Christian ministry.

On the institutional level, the ministerial structure officially and visibly suffered no further changes; the three-fold hierarchy which established itself throughout the Church by the end of the second century, when the bishop was still sometimes called *presbyter*, is met with in all the canonical and liturgical texts of this period. *The Apostolic Tradition* (beginning of the third century) recalls the traditional rules to be observed on the occasion of the ordination of bishops, presbyters, and deacons:

Let the bishop be ordained [being in all things without fault] chosen by all the people. And when he has been proposed and found acceptable to all, the people shall assemble on the Lord's day together with the presbytery and such bishops as may attend. With the agreement of all let the bishops lay hands on him and the presbytery stand by in silence (i. 1–3).

And when a presbyter is ordained, the bishop shall lay his hand upon his head, the presbyter also touching him. And he shall pray over him according to the aforementioned form which we gave before over the bishop. . . (viii. 1).

And a deacon when he is appointed shall be chosen according to what has been said before, the bishop [*alone*] laying hands on him [*in the* same manner]. Nevertheless we order that the bishop alone shall lay on hands at the ordination of a deacon for this reason: that he is not ordained for a priesthood, but for the service of the bishop that he may do [*only*] the things commanded by him (ix. 1; E.T., *The Apostolic Tradition of Hippolytus*, text and tr. ed. and tr. by G. Dix, rev. by H. Chadwick, 1968, pp. 2–3, 13, 15).

In fact this apparent stability of the threefold hierarchy characterised by an ordination with the laying-on-of-hands must not be allowed to obscure the continuing evolution of the ministerial structure to meet new needs in the Church; for this is the way that traditional ministerial roles changed and new ministries arose.

Towards the end of the second century, and during the third, the episcopate changed considerably. Certainly its monarchical authority had already been affirmed in the letters of Ignatius of Antioch. Nothing could officially be done in the Christian community without the bishop's agreement, whether it was the celebration of the eucharist or the marriage of two Christians. But what gave to this authority still more weight from this period onwards was the financial oversight of the community's funds, which allowed the bishop to come to the help of widows and the poor and to pay the Church's ministers. This second responsibility was laden with consequences: henceforward a situation of economic dependence was going to affect the relationship of ministers with their bishop, a relationship which was to become comparable with that of an employer with his workers. This power-relationship was going to play its part in the relationship with civic authorities. Leaving aside times of persecution — which were in any case unusual and often local — political authority always had an interest in gaining the support of a man who enjoyed real political and financial power, and that was well before the rise of Constantine. We find the same sociological pheonomenon of estimating the relative power of bishops in the episcopate itself, which was beginning to build an interior hierarchy.

> It is an observable fact that the authority of bishops of large town does not depend on the apostolic foundation of their churches but is proportionate to the town's importance on a political and economic level. In each province authority is held by the bishop of the civil metropolis, and when people are displeased with him they go over his head to the bishops of the cities of the Empire with the greatest prestige: Rome, Alexandria, Ephesus, Carthage. . . (P. Nautin, art cit. p. 52).

As far as the local church is concerned, the presbyters tended to be overlooked while the deacons played more and more important roles. We see from *The Didascalia,* or *Teaching of the Twelve Apostles* (c. AD 230–250) that the presbyters are no longer chosen by the community, but nominated by the bishop: they surround the bishop, as his counsellors, but their function becomes more and more honorary as they become, relatively speaking, more numerous (46 of them at Rome in about AD 250). The bishop in fact prefers to have recourse to the services of the deacons, whose number often remains limited to seven, in remembrance of the institution of the Seven (Acts 6). These deacons are the mouthpiece and the ears of the bishop.

They concern themselves with the administration and inform 'the bishop about what ought to be done' (*Ap. Trad.*, 8). It is they who attend to the distribution of aid to the poor; and when any Christian wants to pass on anything to the bishop he has to do it through the deacon as intermediary. Practically speaking the deacons, who receive the same salary as the presbyters, enjoy far wider influence. On the other hand, the deaconesses (evidence for whose ministry comes only from the East) tend to disappear because their activity is limited to responsibility for the women of the community.

If the three 'traditional' ministries preserve their importance, the growth of the local churches encourages the creation of new forms of ministry in the churches of the end of the second century. Thus the *Apostolic Tradition* tells us about the appointment of *readers* and *sub-deacons*:

> The reader is appointed by the bishop's handing to him the book. For he does not have hands laid upon him (xii).

> Hands shall not be laid on a subdeacon but he shall be named that he may serve the deacon (xiv; E.T.; op. cit. (Dix, rev. Chadwick), p.21).

There is more precise information from Eusebius of Caesarea (AD 265–340) quoting a letter of Cornelius, bishop of Rome, starting from the official list of those who receive a regular stipend from that church:

> . . . there were 46 presbyters, 7 deacons, 7 sub-deacons, 42 acolytes, 52 exorcists, readers, and janitors, and over 1500 widows and persons in distress, all of whom the grace and kindness of the Master nourish (Eusebius. *H.E.* VI.43.11; E.T.,

Library of Nicene and Post-Nicene Fathers, n.s., vol. 1, 1890, p.288).

This simple enumeration shows how far the ministerial structure of the great churches had become complicated by this time. It was the normal consequence of the growth of the Christian community. Thus it is estimated that towards the middle of the third century there were about 50,000 Christians at Rome for every million inhabitants. Parallel to this evolution of the ministry, two lines of thought were developing which would profoundly influence the subsequent conception of the Christian ministry. The first was already there in Clement of Rome but was going to be developed especially by St Irenaeus, bishop of Lyons, at the end of the second century: that was the idea of apostolic succession. In order to make the authority of the Corinthian presbyters more firm, Clement of Rome had recalled how and by whom they had been admitted to office:

> Now our apostles, thanks to our Lord Jesus Christ, knew that there was going to be strife over the title of bishop. It was for this reason and because they had been given an accurate knowledge of the future, that they appointed the officers we have mentioned. Furthermore, they later added a codicil to the effect that, should these die, other approved men should succeed to their ministry. In the light of this, we view it as a breach of justice to remove from their ministry those who were appointed either by them [i.e., the apostles] or later on and with the whole church's consent, by others of the proper standing . . . (Clement of Rome. *Letter to the Corinthians* XLIV.1-3; E.T., *Library of Christian Classics*, vol. 1, ed. and tr. C.C. Richardson, 1953, pp.63-4).

The problem which faced St Irenaeus was slightly different; it was a question of knowing where true teaching had been preserved, in order to defend it better against gnostic ideas. Irenaeus recognized this true teaching in the great churches, and in particular in the church at Rome, because he could draw up the list of bishops who had succeeded one another in the teaching of 'the true *gnosis*', by which he meant the apostles' teaching:

> True knowledge is that which consists in the doctrine of the apostles and the ancient constitution of the church throughout all the world, and the distinctive manifestation of the body of Christ according to the successions of the bishops, by which they have handed down that church which exists in every place (Irenaeus. *adv. haer*. IV.33.8; E.T., *Ante-Nicene Christian Library*, vol. V.ii, 1880, p.11).

> Wherefore it is incumbent to obey the presbyters who are in the church — those who, as I have shown, together with the succession of the episcopate, have received the certain gift of truth, according to the good pleasure of the Father (ibid., IV.26.2; E.T., *Ante-Nicene Christian Library*, vol. V.i, 1880, p. 462).

It is apparent that the idea of apostolic succession in Irenaeus has the essential purpose of being the guarantee of the authenticity of the teaching of the Word of God. Just as in the teaching of the rabbinic tradition, and as the gnostics also claimed, it was necessary to establish uninterrupted succession from master to disciple in order to ensure the faithfulness of the teaching; a succession which, in the Pastoral Epistles, was expressed by Paul's laying hands on Timothy.

However, by Irenaeus's time, the practice of the Church by which a bishop did not ordain his successor -- who was, in fact, ordained by the bishops of the region round about — contradicted the strict interpretation of this idea of apostolic succession, since the 'master' did not ordain the 'disciple' who was to succeed him. Irenaeus avoids this difficulty by demonstrating that it is the local church, and not only the bishop, who is the guardian of orthodoxy. This is an important nuance: Irenaeus's idea of apostolic succession is different from that of Clement of Rome, who was only concerned with the legitimacy of the institution of the ministers. These two views seem finally to be brought together by Tertullian, who declares, speaking about heretics:

> But if any heresies venture to plant themselves in the apostolic age, so that they may be thought to have been handed down by the apostles because they existed in their time, we can say, Let them examine the origins of their churches, let them unroll the list of their bishops, coming down from the beginning by succession in such a way that their first bishop had for his originator or predecessor one of the apostles or apostolic men; one, I mean, who continued with the apostles. For this is how the apostolic churches record their origins. The church of Smyrna, for example, reports that Polycarp was placed there by John, the church of Rome that Clement was ordained by Peter (Tertullian. *de praescr. haer.* XXXII.1-2; E.T., *Library of Christian Classics*, vol. 5, ed. and tr. S.L. Greenslade, 1956, pp. 52-3).

The second current which flows in the Church from this time on is the use, ever more widely spreading, of *sacerdotal vocabulary* when speaking of the bishop (and, in the following period, of the presbyters). There appear to be two reasons for the rise of this manner of speaking, which is not found in the New Testament: references back to the Old Testament, and parallels with contemporary pagan priesthood.

Ever since the *Letter of Clement of Rome* the organization of the ministry of the New Israel had been compared with that of the old; yet it was no more than a comparison. The *Apostolic Tradition*, however, exactly identifies the episcopal charge with the high-priesthood of the Old Testament; and the ordination prayer proposed for a bishop is perfectly clear about it:

> Father 'who knowest the hearts [*of all*] ' grant upon this thy servant whom thou hast chosen for the episcopate to feed thy holy flock and serve as thine high priest, that he may minister blamelessly by night and day, that he may unceasingly [*behold and*] propitiate thy countenance and offer to thee the gifts of thy holy church, and that by the high priestly spirit he may have authority 'to forgive sins' according to thy command. . . (iii. 4; E.T., op. cit. (Dix, rev. Chadwick), p. 5).

This identification of the ministry of the Church with priesthood has already been expounded by Tertullian, who was at this time probably influenced by the comparison with the official exercise of the pagan priesthood. Indeed, when he attacks the anarchy which, according to him, reigns among the heretics, he declares:

> So one man is bishop today, another tomorrow. The deacon of today is tomorrow's reader, the priest of today is tomorrow a layman. For they impose

priestly functions even upon laymen (Tertullian. *de praescr. haer.* XLI. 8; E.T., *Library of Christian Classics,* vol. 5, ed. and tr. S. L. Greenslade, 1956, p. 62).

Given Tertullian's legal education, this reference to the official functions of the pagan priesthood is not surprising, but we must notice that this comparison can be very easily explained sociologically. To ordinary people, Christian or not, the bishop appeared in the first place as someone who presided over the official acts of prayer, over worship and the eucharist, and by virtue of this played a part analogous to that of the pagan priesthood.

This sacerdotal current became stronger as the third century went on. Towards 250 the letters of St Cyprian, bishop of Carthage, show to what degree the Levitical priesthood of the Old Testament now colours the idea of the Christian ministry. He writes about the presbyter Geminius Faustinus:

> I and my colleagues who were present with me were greatly disturbed, dearest brethren, as were also my fellow-presbyters who sat with us, when we were made aware that Geminius Victor, our brother, when departing this life, had named Geminius Faustinus the presbyter executor to his will, although long since it was decreed, by a council of the bishops, that no one should appoint any of the clergy and the ministers of God executor or guardian by his will, since everyone honoured by the divine priesthood, and ordained in the clerical service, ought to serve only the altar and sacrifices, and to have leisure for prayers and supplications (Cyprian, *Ep.* LXV, *Ante-Nicene Christian Library*, vol. 8, 1876, p. 229; *Ep.* I. i, *CSEL*. III. ii, 1868, p. 465).

This use of the sacerdotal vocabulary is also accompanied by a certain number of titles given to the bishop, particularly that of 'papa' (Father) which expresses filial respect.

So, little by little, when people talked of the Church's ministries, a language very different from that used in the New Testament was developing. No doubt it resulted from the wish to become involved with the Mediterranean society of the time, but the risk was great that fidelity to the gospel conception of the ministry might be lost.

The fourth century was an important turning-point in the legal status of the Church in the heart of the Roman Empire. We move from the Edict of Milan 313, which recognized freedom of worship, to the Edict of Thessalonika 381, by which Theodosius imposed on 'all the peoples of the Empire the religion of Peter the Apostle'.

Following upon this official recognition the Church organizes itself more and more on the lines of the civil administration. Step by step the move is from the idea of ministries in the Church to the organizing of an administration for the believers. Each local church no doubt continues to enjoy a certain autonomy, but this is more and more circumscribed and controlled by a wider system of organization (province = metropolitical see, and patriarchate). The ecumenical council itself, the institution of which first appeared during this epoch, was more or less conceived of and run as a sort of senate of the empire for religious questions; and pressure from the central government, especially from the emperor, was considered quite normal there. The bishops, in fact, could only preserve a measure of autonomy against imperial authority, even in matters concerning the statements of faith, by relying on the support of their local communities. In this context it was of the utmost importance that the local churches should succeed in maintaining their right to choose their bishops for themselves.

State control of the ministry of the Church was no imaginary danger at this time: the clergy, in as much as they were State officials, see themselves being granted a certain number of privileges; in 346 the Emperor even goes so far as to exempt them from the land-tax. Their assimilation to the pagan priesthoods shows itself in the writings of imperial legislators. The clerical caste has achieved a privileged position and an interesting career.

In order to exclude undesirables from the ranks of the clergy, the Councils laid down conditions necessary for ordination and imposed rules about age, suitability, and life-style. These rules could vary from one province to another. We see this in particular over the forbidding of marriage to members of the clergy, or of sexual relations between spouses if their marriage had taken place before the husband's ordination (Council of Elvira, canon 33). There is no point here in going into all the details of this legislation for the *clerical society*, which was becoming increasingly an enclosed world distinct from the mass of the faithful.

The dynamic force in the Christian people indeed showed itself in new ways; this was the period when *monasticism* developed. The monk in principle leaves everything in order to try to live in accordance with all the gospel precepts, and especially to give himself to prayer. The monks therefore shunned most of all ecclesiastical honours and responsibilities. But the Christian flock will often put pressure on these spiritually-minded men to compel them to accept ecclesial ministries and recall once more the demands of the Gospel. So the great Fathers of the Church in the fourth century, like St John Chrysostom and St Basil, had lived for some time at least the monastic life before being called to their episcopal work. In a few exceptional cases, like that of St Ambrose of Milan, another path to this charge could be the exercise of high administrative responsibility with justice and equity. The bishops of the fourth century were both administrators and teachers. The first aspect has been well described by St Ambrose in his *de officiis ministrorum*, a parallel to Cicero's treatise on civil administration; while the second is admirably set out by John *Chrysostom* (which could be translated 'golden-tongued') in his work *de sacerdotio*:

> When all is said and done, there is only one means and only one method of treatment available, and that is teaching by word of mouth. That is the best instrument, the best diet, and the best climate. It takes the place of medicine and cautery and surgery. Without it all else is useless (*de sacerdotio*, IV, 3; E.T., *Saint John Chrysostom: Six Books on the Priesthood*, tr. Graham Neville, 1964, p. 115).

One of the essential functions of the bishop during this period was to teach plainly, to preach and especially to comment on and to explain Holy Scripture. If he is incapable of fulfilling this task himself, he delegates it to one of his priests whom he judges the most capable. In addition, the bishop is the head of the local Christian community which has chosen him, sometimes against his will (e.g., Ambrose at Milan); this choosing strengthens the bond between the community and its bishop who enjoys a sure moral authority.

At the heart of the life of the local church, the

fourth century sees a change in the opposite direction from the third century as far as the position of presbyter against deacon is concerned. In fact there is a vigorous reaction by the presbyters against the growing influence of the deacons. Saint Jerome is a valuable witness of this reaction:

> . . . I am told that someone has been mad enough to put deacons before presbyters, that is, before bishops. For when the apostle teaches clearly that presbyters are the same as bishops, must not a mere server of tables and of widows be insane to set himself up arrogantly over men through whose prayers the body and blood of Christ are made?. . . Their paucity makes deacons persons of consequence, while presbyters are less thought of, owing to their great numbers. But even in the church of Rome the deacons stand while the presbyters seat themselves, although bad habits have by degrees so far crept in that I have seen a deacon, in the absence of the bishop, seat himself among the presbyters, and at social gatherings give his blessing to them. Those who act thus must learn that they are wrong. . . (Jerome. *Letter* 146; E.T., *Library of Christian Classics*, vol. 5, ed. and tr. S. L. Greenslade, 1956, p.387).

This reaction against excessive pretensions results in a very detailed codifying of the deacons' duties and their limits (see Council of Nicea, canon 18; *Apostolic Tradition*, xi. 2–3, op. cit. (Dix, rev. Chadwick, p. 15). Indeed, this reaction will, in the long run, give rise to the *disappearance of the diaconate* as a living ministry, at least in the Latin Church.

Finally, the most fundamental change is certainly found in a weakening of the autonomy of the local churches and a progressive turning of their ministers into *functionaries*. The canons of the Councils are quasi-official witnesses to this transformation. So, in 314, the Council of Arles ordains that presbyters or deacons who leave the Church where they have been ordained are 'deposed' (canon 21). This canon was ratified a little later at Chalcedon, but in a rather different context:

Canon 5. Concerning bishops or clergymen who go about from city to city, it is decreed that the canons enacted by the Holy Fathers shall still retain their force.

Canon 6. Neither presbyter, deacon, nor any of the ecclesiastical order shall be ordained at large nor unless the person ordained is particularly instituted to a church in a city or village, or to a martyry, or to a monastery. And if any have been ordained without a charge, the Holy Synod decrees, to the reproach of the ordainer, that such an ordination shall be inoperative, and that such shall nowhere be suffered to officiate.

Canon 7. We have decreed that those who have once been enrolled among the clergy, or have been made monks, shall accept neither a military charge nor any secular dignity; and if they shall presume to do so and not repent in such wise as to turn again to that which they had first chosen for the love of God, they shall be anathematized.

Canon 10. But if anyone has heretofore been removed from one church to another, he shall not intermeddle with the affairs of his former church (E.T., *Library of Nicene and Post-Nicene Fathers*, n.s., vol. 14, 1900, pp. 271-2, 275).

These canons reveal a great deal, both in what they say and, above all, in what they take for granted. No doubt, in principle, transfers from one church to another continue to be forbidden; but the reality has become so common that there has to be a further precise statement as to the conditions upon which it was acceptable. The minister has become a sort of civil servant who obtains promotion by changing his appointment, and canon 7 shows clearly that in the opinion of the public, the clerical caste forms part of the public administration in the same way as the civil service or the army.

Thus the Christian ministry seemed so much part of imperial society that the ministers became no doubt very useful members of it; but at the same time they ran the risk of being unable to make people feel the gospel's challenge.

The fall of the western Empire under the attacks of the barbarians marks the end of a certain type of society. The new one which will be born out of the ruins and ashes is slowly going to organize itself on the feudal model. The organization of the ecclesial ministry, which had been so strongly integrated into the life of the Empire, is going to undergo a new transformation to adapt itself to this situation.

The civilization of the Roman Empire — and perhaps it is even more true for the Byzantine Empire — was essentially an urban civilization. That of the succeeding period was markedly more rural. The country-dwellers, those *pagani* (= pagans), were slowly evangelized, often through the work of the monasteries whose civilizing and missionary role was considerable at this period. From then on, each of these rural 'parishes' will have a priest at its head; he has not been chosen by the community but, usually, by the bishop or by some influential person. In fact, the priest is very dependent on the 'founder' of the parish, often the owner of an estate, soon the 'lord' of the fief. This 'patron' in practice retains the right to nominate the priest who is to be responsible for the parish he has founded; most frequently the priest lives by the gifts and alms of the faithful; but gradually a real parish endowment comes into being. More than that, in spite of conciliar condemnations, the practice grows of making an offering to the parish priest on the occasion of certain services or religious ceremonies: baptism, burial . . . and there is a rapid slide from a voluntary offering to a sort of scaled tariff. The country priests sometimes regroup themselves round an 'archpriest' (the title appears in the sixth century) who is at the head of a parish where there are several clerks. A little later on, in the Carolingian period, 'deans' appear, a stage between the bishop and the priests, who call the clergy together for meetings for prayer or discussions about doctrine, and pass on the bishop's decisions or citations.

Obviously, the parish priest's task was first of all to celebrate the mass each Sunday and to preach during it. The pulpit indeed often takes the place of an official newspaper, for the parish priest announces there the bishop's — or even the Emperor's — directives. The priest also presides at weddings and funerals, and ensures that the catechism is learned. On weekdays he has a good deal of freedom; so, provided that he does not go hunting or engage in worldly amusements, he can concern himself with teaching the village children and directing a parochial school. Thus he appears as the man of cult and culture. But the culture that he props up is the traditional Latin culture; now at this period the different national languages are appearing, and Latin is no longer understood by the people. So the faithful therefore no longer take a direct part in the celebration of the eucharist and have to be content with 'following' or 'assisting at' it. Henceforward there is a *rupture between clerks and laity*, and we see:

a definite lessening of the active participation of the laity in the realm of the sacred actions, which tend to become more the preserve of a particular order, of the clergy. The canon of the mass is said in a low tone, the faithful do not bring their offerings to the altar any more; in place of the simple *qui offerunt* (who offer) of the Canon, is said *pro quibus tibi offerimus vel qui tibi offerunt* (on whose behalf we offer you, or who offer you); in the ninth century, communion given into the mouth replaces communion given into the hands. . . (Y. Congar, *Revue de droit canonique*, xxiii (1973), p. 87).

The bishops of this period enjoy considerable moral authority; at the time of the barbarian invasions they appear as the defenders of civilization. But they will gradually link themselves to the new feudal system which is growing up; thus Charlemagne is himself going to nominate the bishops, to give them instructions and control them as though they were simply servants of the Crown.

Bishop as liege of the emperor, priest as liege of his 'lord', this feudalism among the Church's ministers is going to extend further and further and in particular to show itself in the field of the administration of ecclesiastical property. A royal edict in France of 779 makes tithe an obligation; the priest becomes director of a financial organisation, of a source of income; his parish is thought of more and more as a 'benefice', valued because of the size of the tithe which it produced.

The close of the Dark Ages saw the spread of simony and of Nicolaitanism. The first abuse, simony, consisting of the purchase of an act of worship with money, arose from the new system of 'benefices'. The bishop paid for his see, the priest in order to assure himself the income of a benefice, the faithful for the sacraments: baptism, marriage, masses. . . In this context, Nicolaitanism, failure to respect the law of celibacy, was a recognized fact and an accepted custom. In spite of ecclesiastical canons demanding continence of the clergy, the number of married priests was considerable, and real priestly dynasties came into being. A parish sometimes became inherited property like any other estate of feudal society, and the Church was obliged to remind people that a special dispensation was necessary for the ordination of a priest's son.

Parallel with the encroachment of feudalism into the Church's ministry, there was a growth of *sacerdotalism in the monasteries*. The Benedictines, whose monasteries by this time possess a considerable influence, are practically all ordained priests without any pastoral responsibility; and the custom takes root in the abbeys of celebrating what were called 'private' masses. This again emphasizes the idea of the priest as the man concerned with the mass and the sacrifice, without attachment to the Christian community.

This picture of the Church's ministry in the Dark Ages is of course very summary; but it does allow us to see the danger which threatens the Church. The Christian ministry is in process of losing its individuality and being practically assimilated to the pagan priesthood or to that of the Old Testament. The ministers have so thoroughly integrated themselves into the movements of feudal society that they lack the strength to react against its abuses.

The quarrel between priesthood and empire, which lasts throughout the eleventh century and ends at Canossa (1077) with the resounding affirmation of the superiority of the pope over the emperor, is going to make deep scars on the relationship of the Church's ministers with feudal society. The clergy become aware of their strength and begin to assert their independence of the political rulers upon whom they were dependent. In 1059, Nicholas II decrees: 'that no priest or clerk must receive a church from a layman's hands, whether given freely or for money'. This reform resulted in the development of papal authority; if clerks are less dependent on lords or emperors, on the other hand they have to obey the pope who lays down rules and sanctions and to whom it is always possible to appeal from any point of medieval Christendom.

When the monk Hildebrand was elected pope in 1073 under the name of Gregory VII, the struggle against simony and Nicolaitanism entered a new phase.

> Assimilating to concubinage, even to fornication, the case of the priest who was married before ordination, and commanding the married priests to send away their wives under pain of being no longer allowed to celebrate the sacraments and of losing their benefices, Gregory VII threatened to suspend bishops who tolerated that priests, deacons, or subdeacons should live with their wives. The same pope and various councils had even forbidden the laity to hear mass said by a married priest. . . (Congar, op.cit, p. 85).

Among a certain number of official decisions, the

council of Clermont presided over by Urban II, decreed in 1095:

> No one is to purchase any ecclesiastical dignity... No recompense is to be demanded for burial or extreme unction. . . Any priest or bishop living unchastely is to be deposed... Priests' sons will not be admitted to ecclesiastical charges or dignities, but may become monks.

On the positive side, this draconian reform was linked with the development of *canons regular,* whose way of quasi-monastic common life made the observance of consecrated celibacy more easy. Thus Nicholas II decreed as early as 1059:

> We require and ordain that clerks-in-holy-orders, priests, deacons, and sub-deacons, live together near the churches to which they have been ordained. They should share a common refectory and dormitory; and we beg and warn them to apply themselves to the practice of the Apostles' way of life in all its perfection.

The Gregorian reform deeply marked the Western Church, but did not reach the Eastern Church at all; during this period the Eastern Church is asserting its independence of Rome. Through the energetic action of the popes and Councils the reform went rapidly into effect and especially transformed the relationships between the Church's ministers and the secular authorities, bringing about an indisputable renaissance of Christianity in western Europe. However, these measures henceforward link the exercise of any ministry in the Church to a more or less monastic life-style, essentially characterized by celibacy. No doubt such a link between ecclesial ministry and this particular way of life was no novelty: it marks the outcome of a process which had been going on for several centuries; but the Gregorian reform institutionalized it to such an extent that it has become in practice a condition of the validity of the ecclesial ministry.

In the thirteenth century Western Europe was obviously in a state of economic and social change. Unrest among the peasants, the ending of the Crusades, the development of universities, the building of cathedrals, are the more visible signs of that cultural and social ferment. The Church and her ministries take a direct part in this evolution, most particularly by the creating of new religious orders, the Dominicans and the Franciscans. As far as these movements are concerned, the apostolic way of life takes priority over monasticism, the ministry of the Word over formal worship. Further, in a society awakening to international relationships these religious, for the most part ordained priests, will care about preaching the gospel and will wander over the earth for that purpose, if need be. They were attempting to replace the armed crusade by conversion to the gospel through the preaching of the Word.

These new religious orders must not, however, make us forget that the majority of the Church's ministers, bishops, priests, or inferior clerks are still 'seculars', and that they continue to carry out their functions, which are centred on public worship; the priests are thought of essentially as celebrants of the mass. Even though some of them have studied theology or canon law in the new universities, the main task of the priesthood remains the celebration of the mass in Latin, in a language no longer understood by the people, and at an altar which was placed further and further distant from the lay people present. In fact, there are too many priests, and many of them no longer have any pastoral responsibility. They live by celebrating masses, by being given or by purchasing a benefice, or on their own private income. Nevertheless the number of parishes is increasing, especially in the towns where population is growing. A real hierarchy comes into being among the priests in any diocese: vicars-general, archpriests, deans, incumbents, curates, chaplains. . . This organization witnesses to an attempt to adapt the Church's structures to an evolving society; but it will also lead to greater inequalities between priests, particularly on the material level.

The idea of the ecclesial minister as essentially a cultic figure is clearly seen in the theology of this period. It takes for granted the use of sacerdotal terms, and defines a priest as one who has the power to celebrate the mass; and from this point of view, makes very little of the distinction between priest and bishop, since both have the same power of consecrating the eucharist. Some texts from the treatise on the sacrament of holy orders in the *Summa Theologiae* clearly demonstrate this way of thinking: if they are not in fact the direct work of St Thomas Aquinas they are more or less evidence of the theology normally taught in the universities:

This sacrament consists above all else in the delegation of a power. . . the priest [*sacerdos*] has two functions: the first, the principal one, has for its object the body of Christ; the other, secondary, the mystical body of Christ. This second function depends on the first, and they are not reciprocal. For many are vowed to the priesthood to whom only the first function is given; for example, religious, who do not have the cure of souls. . . the principal end of the power of Holy Orders is the consecration of the body of Christ, its distribution to the faithful, and the forgiveness of sins promised to the faithful. . . Those who receive the sacrament of Holy Order are therefore set over the faithful: they must be first by the merits of their holy lives. . . Orders cannot be received more than once, for in each order a character is implanted. . . the power is given to the priest at the moment of his being handed the chalice. . . the episcopate is not a separate order, if by that word we understand a sacrament.

The crisis of the sixteenth century Reformation occurs in the context of a European society which is once again in a process of profound change, and also — what is most important — in a Church where abuses among its ministers are increasingly strident. Less and less do its priests have a cure of souls, incumbents are very often absent from their parishes; clerks amass benefices without the formality of being ordained, the pope himself appears more as a political power than a religious leader.

This historical setting explains the necessity for a reformation directed above all towards the ministries. The reform proposed by Luther is radical because it rejects sacerdotal language and the distinction 'priest-layman':

It is pure invention that pope, bishop, priests, and monks are called the spiritual estate while princes, lords, artisans, and farmers are called the temporal estate. This is indeed a piece of deceit and hypocrisy. Yet no one need be intimidated by it, and for this reason: all Christians are truly of the spiritual estate, and there is no difference among them except that of office. . . As far as that goes, we are all consecrated priests through baptism, as St Peter says in 1 Peter 2, 'You are a royal priesthood and a priestly realm. . .'. Suppose a group of earnest Christian laymen were taken prisoner and set down in a desert without an episcopally ordained priest among them. And suppose they were to come to a common mind there and then in the desert and elect one of their number, whether he were married or not, and charge him to baptize, say mass, pronounce absolution, and preach the gospel. Such a man would be as truly a priest as though he had been ordained by all the popes and bishops in the world. . . Therefore a priest in Christendom is nothing else but an officeholder. As long as he holds office he takes precedence; where he is deposed he is a peasant or a townsman like anybody else. Indeed a priest is never a priest when he is deposed (Martin Luther. *To the Christian nobility of the German nation concerning the reform of the Christian estate* (1520); E.T., *Luther's Works*, American edn, vol. 44, ed. J. Atkinson, Philadelphia 1966, pp. 128-9).

This fundamental declaration, as much with Luther as with Calvin, is accompanied by the affirmation that it is useful for the Church to have true pastors whose principal task is emphasized — that of the ministry of the Word firmly based on study and exegesis of holy Scripture.

Such a conception of the ministry was diametrically opposed to the 'sacerdotal' idea officially taught in the universities, whose essential features we have seen above. Indeed, this official 'sacerdotal' theology is repeated, with a few slight changes, in the decrees of Session 23 of the Council of Trent (1563):

Canon 1. If anyone says that in the New Testament

70

there is no visible and outward priesthood, or that there is no power to consecrate and offer the true body and blood of the Lord, to remit or retain sins, but there is only a charge [*officium*] and a simple ministry of preaching the Gospel; or that those who do not preach are not priests [*sacerdotes*] : let him be anathema.

Canon 2. If anyone says that, apart from the priesthood, there are no other orders in the Catholic Church, major or minor, by which one approaches the priesthood as by degrees; let him be anathema.

Canon 4. If anyone says that in holy Ordination the Holy Spirit is not given, and that it is vain for the bishops to say: Receive the Holy Spirit; or that by ordination an indelible character is not imprinted, or that a man once ordained priest [*sacerdos*] can revert to the lay state; let him be anathema.

Canon 6. If anyone says that there is no hierarchy instituted by divine intention in the Catholic Church, comprising bishops, priests [*presbyteris*] and other ministers; let him be anathema.

Canon 7. If anyone says that bishops are not superior to priests [*presbyteris*] and do not possess the power to confirm and ordain, or that what they possess is in common with the priests [*presbyteris*] ; or that orders conferred by them are invalid without the consent of or a call by the people or the secular power; or that those who have not been ordained by ecclesiastical, canonical authority, nor sent out by them, but have their origin elsewhere, are truly ministers of the Word and Sacraments; let him be anathema.

These canons of the Council of Trent deserve a detailed commentary; it is clear that they must be understood as the taking up of an official position by the Church in a very precise historical context, in response to a challenge which belongs to that period and in a polemical climate which must not be ignored. All through these canons, one senses that the Fathers of the council wanted essentially to reaffirm *the necessity of the Church's having a structure* and having true ministers. We shall return, in our chapter where we think generally about the ministry, to these decrees of the Council of Trent. However we can at this point stress the vocabulary used; canons 1–4 employ 'sacerdotal' language (*sacerdotes* in canon 1), while canons 6–7 speak of the priest by the ancient term *presbyter*; this double language is also found in the second Vatican council, and we shall try to understand what it implies.

In fact the preoccupations of the Council of Trent were as much pastoral as they were theological, and the council Fathers issued decrees giving a certain amount of concrete guidance relating to the training and ordination of candidates for the ministry, about the material support and the life-style of priests. Thus the bishop is recommended to ordain priest only those who can obtain a benefice or have a sufficient private income (that is done in order to avoid the clergy's becoming beggars); and the parish priests to attend to the religious training of their faithful, through preaching. Recommendations about life-style even go into details about clothing (forbidding silk, and coloured shoes!). Generally speaking, 'in clothing, behaviour, conversation, and in all else, clerks must exhibit only what is grave and modest, full of religion. . .'.

But the most important aspect of the directives, the one which has most lastingly marked the Church's ministers down to our day, is certainly the setting-up of *seminaries*. In June 1546, the Council Fathers showed their anxiety to ensure a proper preparation for clerics:

> In churches where the annual income is too small, where the number of the faithful and of the members of the clergy is so few that the teaching of theology cannot suitably take place, let there be at least a master chosen by the bishop, with the advice of the Chapter, to teach grammar to the clerks and to the other poor scholars without fee, so that they may go on from that, by God's good grace, to the study of Holy Scripture.

But it was only in 1563, at the time when it was replying to Luther's theses and reaffirming the necessity for structures in the Church, that the Council promulgated the decree on seminaries. Henceforward, every bishop will have to found a college receiving, for preference, poor children and preparing them to be ministers of the Church through a serious training; initiating them into grammar, to plainchant, to the liturgical calendar, to holy Scripture, to the sermons of the Fathers. . . . This decree was rapidly applied in Italy and Spain, and in France too — particularly from the seventeenth century. Under the influence of Monsieur Vincent (St Vincent de Paul) and of Monsieur Olier, who founded specialist associations of priests, Lazarists and Sulpicians, to staff the seminaries, houses for preparation for the priesthood and associations of priests multiply. A 'sacerdotal' spirituality develops, especially in the Sulpician tradition; its fundamental direction relies upon the recommendation from the liturgy of Ordination: 'Carry out in your life what you accomplish at the altar'. It lays stress on the priest's spiritual life, but starting from a sacerdotal theory centred on the altar it develops the individualistic tendencies of the clergy, and does little enough for the pastoral thinking of the future leaders of the community.

This period sees the rise of a number of religious orders, especially missionary orders; among these, the Jesuits occupy a special place. Almost contemporary with the Council of Trent, this Order will be one of the most effective instruments of what is called the 'Catholic counter-Reformation'. Religious though they are, the Jesuits have no resemblance to monks; their activity is wholly directed towards apostolic work, whether in western Europe or in what are called 'missionary' lands. Following upon a long and demanding preparation they add to the three traditional vows of religious one of particular obedience to the pope; that is to say, they form a body of specialist ministers in the service of the universal Church. Nevertheless their direct link with the pope and their growing influence in the ruling classes of European society made them the object of suspicion in the eighteenth century, that they served Roman interests rather than those of their own countries; and a certain number of nominally catholic governments ordered their expulsion.

The position of the contemporary Church and that of her ministers varies a good deal from one country to another, from one continent to another. The picture one has of a priest, for example, of his relations with the Christian community or with the civil authorities, differs very much, depending on whether one is thinking of him in a country village, in a large town, in Spain, or in the U.S.A. Yet right up to the second Vatican Council it appeared that the Roman Catholic church continued steadily along the lines set by the Council of Trent as far as the organization of its

74

ministry was concerned; and in the Latin church the seminaries, whether of Rome, Paris, or New York, assured a certain unity of the priest's life-style by giving him a uniform kind of training.

The first Vatican Council (1870), continuing the thought of the Council of Trent, laid especial emphasis on the reaffirmation of the necessity and the powers of the 'hierarchy' in the Church: it laid down above all the authority of the tip of that hierarchy, of the Pope. The definition of papal infallibility, whatever shades of interpretation there may be, is significant of this way of looking at things. Vatican I no doubt intended to speak next of the Christian idea of the other ministries, and especially of that of the bishops; but the accidental suspension of its sittings on account of the political situation had grave consequences at the close of the nineteenth century and the beginning of the twentieth for the normal way of teaching about the Church's ministries. The Church was often presented as a pyramid in which everything depended on the point, that is, on the Pope.

The profound changes which occurred in society and in civilization during the early years of the twentieth century made themselves felt only gradually in the Church, and even less quickly in the minds of the clergy, whose training and life-style had created them as a world apart, shut in upon themselves, with their own special dress; who, whether it was in public worship or in teaching theology, did not speak the same language as ordinary mortals. The urgent need for fundamental reform was obvious, and it was with this in mind that Pope John XXIII summoned the second Vatican Council (1962–5).

In a certain number of its Constitutions and Decrees this Council put forward pastoral and doctrinal directions for the Church of the second half of the twentieth century. In fact the role and mission of the Church's ministers are especially tackled in the dogmatic constitution on the Church (*Lumen Gentium*) and in the decrees on the pastoral responsibilities of the bishops and the ministry and life of priests, but there are also references, no less important in their implications, in other constitutions and decrees.

The dogmatic constitution *Lumen Gentium* is insistent on presenting the Church as 'the people of God' (ch.ii) before it mentions the ministers (ch.iii). This order of priorities indicates a whole theological concept: the ministers (or, as the Council often says, 'the hierarchy') are not put above but *in* the Church, and before dealing with the ministry the Council insists on reaffirming the common priesthood of the faithful, even if its connection with the 'ministerial priesthood' is not yet very clear. (para. 10)

In chapter iii the Council deals directly with 'the hierarchical structure of the Church': 'For the nurturing and constant growth of the People of God, Christ the Lord instituted *in His Church a variety of ministries*, which work for the good of the whole body. For those ministers who are endowed with sacred power are servants of their brethren, so that all who are of the People of God, and therefore enjoy a true Christian dignity, can work toward a common goal freely and in an orderly way, and arrive at salvation' (iii,18). This introduction is of the greatest importance; it reveals a new language ('ministers' instead of 'hierarchy' or 'priesthood') or rather it recovers the language of the New Testament (Eph. 4.11-16). Even if in what follows, the text only deals directly with the bishop's ministry, and in passing with that of priests and deacons — because in fact they are the ministries which exist in the catholic Church today — it is characteristic that the Council wanted from the start to stress the *variety* of ministers. There is a new and very important hypothesis here which will be able to guide us in our essay reflecting generally on this question.

What the Constitution next sets out is essentially the bishop's ministry: 'Among the principal duties of his bishops, the preaching of the gospel occupies an eminent place' (iii,25). To express the relationship of bishop and priests, the Council takes up the idea of *presbyterium* already found in St Ignatius of Antioch: 'Priests, prudent cooperators with the episcopal order as well as its aids and instruments, are called to serve the People of God. They constitute one priesthood with their bishop, although that priesthood is comprised of different functions' (iii,28). Taking up next the 'lower level of the hierarchy', that is to say, the deacons, the Council proposed to renew in its full meaning this ancient order which had for many centuries practically disappeared in the Latin Church: 'The diaconate can in the future be restored as a proper and permanent rank of the hierarchy. It pertains to the competent territorial bodies of bishops, of one kind or another, to decide, with the approval of the Supreme Pontiff, whether and where it is opportune for such deacons to be appointed for the care of souls. With the consent of the Roman Pontiff, this diaconate will be able to be conferred upon men of more mature age, even upon those living in the married state. It may also be conferred upon suitable young men. For them, however, the law of celibacy must remain intact' (iii,29). The Council returns to the duties of bishops and priests in two particular decrees from which it is interesting to extract some fairly new directions: for instance, the collegial responsibility of bishops to the universal

Church: 'each one in concert with his fellow bishops is responsible for the Church' (para. 6); and of the idea of a *local church* to describe a diocese: 'A diocese is that portion of God's people which is entrusted to a bishop to be shepherded by him with the cooperation of the presbytery. Adhering thus to its pastor and gathered together by him in the Holy Spirit through the gospel and the Eucharist, this portion constitutes a *particular* [i.e. local] *church* in which the one, holy, catholic, and apostolic Church of Christ is truly present and operative' (para. 11). Two other paragraphs also deserve mention; one about the independence of bishops from the public authorities, the other on their resignation from their responsibilities: 'In discharging their apostolic office, which concerns the salvation of souls, bishops of themselves enjoy full and perfect freedom and independence from any civil authority' (para. 19). They must then refuse special privileges: 'this most holy Council desires that in the future no rights or privileges of election, nomination, presentation, or designation for the office of bishop be any longer granted to civil authorities' (para. 20). 'Since the pastoral office of bishops is so important and weighty, when diocesan bishops and others, regarded in law as their equals, have become less capable of fulfilling their duties properly because of the increasing burden of age or some other serious reason, they are earnestly requested to offer their resignation from office either on their own initiative or upon invitation from the competent authority' (para. 21). We should notice too that the same rule applies to 'Pastors who are unable to fulfil their office properly and fruitfully because of the increasing burden of age or some other serious reason' (para. 31).

Finally, we must draw attention to a new ministerial

structure, the 'episcopal conferences', whose duties are described in paragraphs 37 and 38.

The decree on the ministry and life of the priest (*Presbyterium Ordinis*) has had a history which is lively and which shows the way in which contemporary theological research on the ministry has developed. The changes in the title itself show that we have passed from a 'clericalized' way of thinking, then to a 'sacerdotal' (with emphasis on life-style), and finally to a 'ministerial and presbyteral' way of thinking which recovers the language of the New Testament and of the first centuries of the Church's history, especially with the use of the term *presbyter*. Even if this evolution is not complete (there remain numerous indications of the 'sacerdotalizing' idea from the first schemata, in particular the poorly thought-out application of the epistle to the Hebrews to the Church's ministries), it seems to us as significant and illuminating for an attempt at theological synthesis today. Among the priest's responsibilities, as with the bishop's, it is the preaching of the gospel which comes first (para. 4); his role in the celebration of the eucharist is intimately linked to his function as president of the community: 'It is the eucharistic assembly which is the centre of the Christian community over which the priest presides' (para. 5). This presentation links immediately with the directions of the constitution of the sacred Liturgy: 'The Church, therefore, earnestly desires that Christ's faithful, when present at this mystery of faith, should not be there as strangers or silent spectators. On the contrary, through a proper appreciation of the rites and prayers they should participate knowingly, devoutly, and actively. They should be instructed by God's word and be refreshed at the table of the Lord's body; they should give thanks to God; by offering the immaculate Victim, not only through the hands of the priest, but also *with him*, they should learn to offer themselves too' (para. 48). From now on the presidential function must not separate the priest from other Christians, nor set him over the community of the faithful, but on the contrary 'priests are *brothers among brothers* with all those who have been reborn at the baptismal font. They are all members of one and the same body of Christ, whose upbuilding is entrusted to us all' (para. 9). Here too, we find phrases close to the Gospels' (see Matt. 23.8).

With this look at the official texts of Vatican II, we end our historical panorama of the way in which the ministries in all their forms have been lived out and interpreted down the Church's history. This panorama, we repeat, is a rapid one, incomplete, scrappy, and thus inevitably biassed; it is impossible to set down in a few pages the story of the ministries of the Church in all its richness. Yet we have been able to emphasise its most important stages, and to notice the way in which in the course of centuries the Church has lived out her ministries. This glance back will help us to understand and appreciate better the fundamental directions and the problems which theological thinking is taking on the ministry today.

3

CHRISTIAN THINKING ABOUT THE
CHURCH'S MINISTRY

The witness of the New Testament and of the Church's life in the course of its long history must be allowed to shed light on the Christian way of understanding and organizing the ministry today. Without such confrontation, particularly with the canonical text of the New Testament, our thinking about the Church's ministers in our day would run the serious risk of missing what is essential, and of letting the Christian ministry lose its original, that is to say, its evangelistic character.

Yet if the Church must remain faithful to herself — that is, to Jesus Christ — this faithfulness must not be thought of as a mere repetition of forms or institutions from her past. The Holy Spirit is at work in the world and in the Church today, as he was yesterday, and he can guide the Church towards an *aggiornamento*, a renewal of the forms and institutions of the past, in order to make the Church a better 'light of the Gentiles' in this present world. Before we can distinguish the calls and questions which will arise for the Church tomorrow, we must therefore take account of the socio-cultural milieu of the world and the Church of today, and of the fundamental points in Christian thinking about the ministries which we can regard as generally accepted.

The modern socio-cultural environment

Granted such a sub-title, we do not claim to offer here a detailed analysis of modern civilization: we shall content ourselves with a reminder of some aspects of it as we see them clearly demonstrated in what we call 'Western society'. In doing this, we are well aware of our limitations: we ought in particular to complete this analysis by examining Eastern and African civilization; but the size of this present study forbids it. Besides, statistically speaking, it is in the so-called Western world that the majority of Christians still live.

It is no completely new phenomenon: human history is also technological history; man has always been *homo faber*. But the gap between man and the world which does not bear his marks, which we call 'Nature', is growing wider and wider. Indeed, the world unmarked by man is tending to disappear totally; to remind himself of its existence modern man creates 'nature reserves'; and interplanetary space itself is no longer out of reach of the civilization of the end of the twentieth century.

The 'holy' has often been presented as the realm which is untouched by human activity; thus it used particularly to consist of natural phenomena which were linked to divine activity: rain, storm, earthquake, birth, fertility. . . Man today lays claim to control all these phenomena, including the reproduction of his own species. No doubt this 'project' is as yet only partly fulfilled; none the less, the domain of 'Nature' and the domain of 'the holy' — which always tended to be more or less confused with each other in the thinking of religious people — are shrinking like a piece of snakeskin. Science and technology do not in principle recognize any reserved areas. Thus Western civilization, in its very axioms, appears 'deconsecrated'; religious feeling no longer knows how to express or to nourish itself, and seems ready to disappear as far as its traditional forms are concerned.

One of the consequences of this technological

civilization is the development of a world built wholly by and for man: the town. It is no longer possible in our day to contain or protect towns by surrounding them with walls; they explode outwards; the huge metropolis of the West becoming a 'megalopolis', holding several millions, then several tens of millions, of people. This phenomenon of urbanization characterizes the nineteenth and even more the twentieth century. We can remind ourselves as an example of the simple fact that France was still very largely rural at the beginning of the present century, and that now more than 70% of her people live in towns.

This change to living in towns has direct consequences not merely on each individual's life-style, but even more on the way in which human relations and communities begin and develop; and thus also affects Christian communities. In a village of a few hundred inhabitants, everyone knows everyone else, everyone knows who is who; in a block of flats in a huge town it often happens that you do not know your neighbour but do develop relationships with people who live in another part of the town. In an urban civilization relationships, and so human communities, are in general more selective, more a matter of choice.

In traditional societies the authority upon which the community's life depends is spontaneously 'consecrated': the anointing of kings and emperors is only one of many indications of what is felt at a much deeper level in the community's life. If the king is king 'by divine right', the father's authority in the family also seems 'by divine right', a sharing in the sacred character of all authority.

People moreover used to talk of 'power' rather than 'authority'. For example, the *code Napoléon* still speaks of 'paternal power' — a phrase changed only in

1970 to 'parental authority'. Commenting on the new law, Monsieur Colombet has expressed the general opinion as to the significance of this change in terminology: 'we no longer have a *power* but an *authority*; and this change in wording corresponds to a change of ethos. The word *power* calls to mind the Roman *potestas*, that is to say, a right, a power of domination. The word *authority* corresponds to a complex of rights and duties, to what we nowadays call a function when speaking of something which is neither simply of right nor of obligation.' (cf. G. Wiederkehr 'L'autorité et sa problématique dans la société civile', *Revue de droit canonique*, xxiii (1973), p. 168).

This change in vocabulary therefore reveals a change in ways of thinking:

> It follows from this that an authority is only licit if it takes a proper place within a juridical system. . . the legitimacy of the authority cannot be determined from any simple, formal viewpoint. If an authority is not legitimate simply because it has been set up by the procedure laid down in law, then it must depend on other sets of values. . . . In other words, authority today must justify itself by the way in which it is exercised (art. cit., pp, 177f).

So, 'parental authority is only given to parents as far as they accept it properly and on the condition that they wield it in the right way' (ibid., p. 180). 'Every authority therefore is continually being called in question' (ibid., p. 182).

It is probably in this context of the evolution of the idea of power into the idea of authority that the development of what we call the democratic way of living can be understood. Power is no longer a natural thing, wielded because you are born into this or that family, yours until death; but since power must be used for the people, the exercise of that power will be under their control. This authority is in fact entrusted to someone for only a limited time and the people decide whether or not to renew it; their decision will depend on their view of the way in which it has been wielded, well or ill. Of course we are talking about an 'ideal', and its realization will differ very much from country to country; moreover, even in the countries regarded as the most democratic, the authority of parents in the family, of the owner in his works, is not always influenced by elections. None the less this *democratic ideal*, influencing the way authority is exercised, has profoundly marked Western society; and life-long positions of responsibility are rarely found there now.

Compared with the ideal of democracy, the ideal of a society where men and women have equal opportunity for responsibility is enshrined very often in statutes but far less often actually applied. In this, things vary greatly from one country to another. It is odd, too, to discover that in a country of traditions, like India, there appears to be no problem about a women's wielding supreme political authority, whereas Western countries like the U.S.A. and France have never known a woman as head of the State.

But whatever the facts of the situation may be, equal rights for men and woman are clearly written in to the United Nations' Universal Declaration of the Rights of Man, and can be found (more or less distinctly written) in the majority of modern codes of law. So in French law, for example, we discover that at the time when the idea of 'paternal power' in the *code Napoléon* was changed to 'parental authority', the idea of 'marital authority' also disappears. In practice the number of professions and responsibilities solely the preserve of men is diminishing every year: 'Women are gaining wider influence in cities, a power which they have never held before' (Pope Paul's message at the end of Vatican II)

Every one of these aspects of our modern world poses a question to the Church about its idea of its ministries. We shall therefore try to take them into account not only in our general essay on the Christian ministry today but also, and perhaps still further, in an evaluation of the still unsolved problems.

Within the Church

There are some aspects of the contemporary Church which touch directly on ecclesial thinking about the ministry for today; let us review them briefly.

With the new influence of the laity, we find a complex phenomenon whose many facets reflect the same truth: *the disappearance of the gulf separating the people of God from their ministers.* In the nineteenth century and then at the beginning of the twentieth century, this separation had reached a disturbing size; the clergy formed a world apart, with its own dress, habits, and language. Christians had the impression that they were diminished, less and less the 'Church'; those who had had no sort of classical education felt more and more that they were foreigners in a Church which did not speak their language. The launching of Catholic Action and of other movements, in which Christians had been called on to take responsibility for evangelizing those around them indeed marked an important turning-point in active sharing by all the baptized in the Church's life. Elsewhere the realization of the gulf which separated the Church (meaning, effectively, the clergy) and the modern world, particularly the working-class world, resulted in several movements which tried to put priests into the life of that world. The appearance of worker-priests was without doubt the most spectacular of these, but we must not underestimate the efforts made to renew links through a liturgy in everyday language.

This phenomenon of 'declericalization' (that is, the ending of the formation by the 'clerics' of a world of their own) has been discussed on the theoretical level and certainly has not come to full bloom in practice. Nevertheless it seems absolutely right when considered sociologically, and probably forms an extremely important event in the life of the Catholic Church in Western Europe.

'Promoting the restoration of unity among all Christians is one of the chief concerns of the Second Sacred Ecumenical Synod of the Vatican' (para. 1). . . 'This sacred Synod, therefore, exhorts all the Catholic faithful to recognize the signs of the times and to participate skillfully in the work of ecumenism' (para. 4). These two quotations from the *Decree on Ecumenism* emphasise the importance of the movement towards unity among the Christian churches during the second half of the twentieth century.

Recognition of ministries figures prominently among the chief questions dividing the different churches, and especially the Roman Catholic Church and the Churches of the Reformation (see *Decree on Ecumenism*, 22). Also since the Council a climate of more brotherly collaboration in pastoral matters among the ministers of the various churches was established on the pastoral level while theologians were striving to understand one another better and to examine their differences in the light of a renewal of theological thought. Let us cite among the conclusions of this ecumenical dialogue:

1 *Ministry and Ordination: a Statement on the Doctrine of the Ministry, agreed by the Anglican-Roman Catholic international Commission,* Canterbury 1973. The booklet from the 'Groupe des Dombes'.

2 *Pour une reconciliation des Ministères: élements d'accord entre catholiques et protestants* (1973); E.T., 'Towards a reconciliation of ministries' in *Modern Ecumenical Documents on the Ministry* (SPCK 1975).

The Anglican-Roman Catholic statement lays special stress on the fact that 'Agreement on the nature of Ministry is prior to the consideration of the mutual recognition of ministries' (para. 17); while the Groupe des Dombes emphasizes that

> The question of ministries being a major obstacle to unity, it is on this point that the change of heart (*metanoia*) of the Church ought primarily to concentrate (para. 38).

Any thinking about the Ministry in today's Church must then take full account of this ecumenical dimension.

Both the demands of the ecumenical dialogue and the effort to renew Christian thought have led theologians to a still more attentive encounter with the source-materials of the Christian faith found in Scripture and in the written tradition. It is solely this kind of encounter which allows us to see the distinction between the essential and the subordinate in the formulas of the Christian faith; between what is 'the word of God' and what is only 'the tradition of men'

(Mark 7.8-9); between the Christian message itself and the forms in which it was presented at this or that period and in these or those circumstances.

The Scriptures play a fundamental role in the deep exploration and drawing of distinctions that is necessary. If the Church from the first centuries has recognized the biblical texts as 'canonical' it was because she was recognizing in these inspired texts an abiding value for her own life. It has been understood ever since that, Sunday by Sunday, she invites Christians to listen again to the fundamental texts which illuminate their lives; and that 'the study of the sacred page is, as it were, the soul of sacred theology' (Constitution *Dei Verbum*, 24).

Now, the reading of the Scriptures during the Sunday assembly in the language spoken in the country, the existence of good translations of the whole Bible, and the advance in the exegesis of the texts permit of a better understanding of this 'word of God'. Theological thinking about the ministries must henceforward take account of this effort to return to our sources, and particularly of the contribution of the biblical renewal.

The problem of 'sacerdotal' language

Words were created in order that we might understand one another. However, it seems that some words are given different meanings by one group and the other; and that other words have a two-fold meaning which can sometimes result in misunderstandings with consequences that are more serious or less so. In this way there are certain words which have played an important part in the Church's history. The terms 'priesthood' and in a more general way 'sacerdotal' language applied to the Church's ministers have caused some fine polemic and in the end have been one of the causes of separation at the Reformation. It is important, then, to clear this matter up before any attempt at synthesis.

The word 'priest' in English is ambiguous. To be convinced of this, we have only to see how it is employed to translate two quite different words from Latin, Greek, and Hebrew:

i   In everyday speech 'priest' most often means the man who has responsibility for celebrating the cult, offering the sacrifices, carrying out the official religious rites. In this sense, 'priest' = *sacerdos* (Latin), *hiereus* (Greek), *cohen* (Hebrew).

ii   But as the dictionaries all remind us, 'priest', etymologically speaking, means 'old man', 'senator', 'elder', member of the responsible council of a community. Here 'priest' = *presbyter* (Latin), *presbuteros* (Greek), *zaqen* (Hebrew), and we can link with this the words *presbytery* (the house where the priest lives), *presbyterium* (the diocesan college of priests), and the adjective *presbyteral*.

This ambiguity in the word 'priest' in modern speech is no etymological accident. It probably reflects the fairly widespread confusion which exists between the sacerdotal and presbyteral ideas. It is the direct result of applying sacerdotal language to particular ministers in the Church and displays the confusion in the use of the Latin words *sacerdos* and *presbyter* in many official or semi-official documents of the Latin Catholic Church. In order to try to see clearly in this confusion, let us briefly remind ourselves of the historical data behind this problem of speech.

i   At the beginning, in the New Testament, there is no confusion whatever: if particular groups of ministers in the Church are called 'priests' or 'presbyters' (*presbyteros* in Greek) it is always in so far as they are members of the presiding body in the Christian community (second meaning, above); the New Testament never employs for Christian ministers the word 'priest' = *hiereus*, in the sacerdotal meaning (first, above).

ii From the end of the second century, influenced by the Old Testament and by the sociological role now played by the president of the liturgical assembly, the title *sacerdos* ('priest', first meaning) was used for the bishops, then for the priests (*presbyters*, second meaning).

iii From the early Middle Ages the eucharistic assembly was normally under the presidency of a 'priest' (*presbyter*); ever since the two words *presbyter* and *sacerdos* are very often used interchangeably, and the latter tends to displace the former.

iv Scholastic theology confirmed the use of sacerdotal language by using the idea of priesthood, *sacerdotium*, as the starting-point in its discussion of the sacrament of Holy Orders.

v In the sixteenth century, Luther's violent reaction against this sort of language called into question the whole ministerial structure of his time.

vi The Council of Trent (see p. 72) did not really appear to understand the problem raised by the use of sacerdotal terms which were current language in the theology of the time; the whole purpose of the Fathers' declaration appeared to be strongly to defend the traditional ministerial structures (and thus it defends even the minor orders. . .), in this way ensuring the unity of the Church and protecting it from anarchy.

vii Until the second Vatican council, Roman Catholic documents very frequently use *sacerdos* instead of *presbyter*.

viii The second Vatican council, influenced by the biblical renewal and by the ecumenical dialogue, generally attempt to distinguish *sacerdos* and *presbyter*. This effort at precision of language may be characteristically seen in the successive titles put forward for the document on the priesthood: *de sacerdotibus* (1963); *de vita et ministerio sacerdotali* (Spring 1964); *de ministerio et vita presbyterorum* (December 1964); *Presbyterorum ordinis* — the title of the final decree.

This historical summary is eloquent: since the use of sacerdotal language has led to ambiguities, and has been one of the causes of disunity among Christians, it seems preferable to us to restrict its use to the very minimum; and to use it only where it is necessary and where no ambiguity can arise. Vatican II shows us the path we must tread, towards clearer precision in the words we use. Instead of saying 'priesthood' it is preferable to say 'presbyterate'; instead of 'sacerdotal' or 'priestly ministry', to say 'presbyteral ministry'.

Such a change in vocabulary will seem pointless to some people. In fact it opens up a whole series of questions in theological discussion and that is why it is unavoidable; we must tackle it before even trying to offer any sort of theological synthesis. Within the framework of 'priestly' language, theologians usually offer their reflections on the ministerial structure of the Church in three steps:

1. The priesthood of Christ
2. The priesthood of the people of God
3. The ministerial priesthood

Now if the first point is clearly developed in the New Testament, especially in the letter to the Hebrews; and the second (often, unhappily, left out) in the first letter of Peter; the 'ministerial priesthood' has no scriptural basis and depends quite simply on theological speculation. On the other hand, by using 'ministerial' language — that of the New Testament — we rediscover two lines of thought vital for the Church. When we speak of *a ministry*, he who performs it must have the spirit of offering *service*; when we talk about *different ministries* there can be a great diversity among ministers.

Moreover, in a world in process of 'secularization', a 'deconsecrated' world, it is obvious that if the priest is thought of as *sacerdos*, that is to say, the cultic figure, the man concerned with the 'holy', his existence is becoming meaningless. On the other hand, if the priest is the leader, the 'resource-man' of a Christian community which is trying to live out the gospel, he may no doubt enquire about the value of this current of 'deconsecration'; but without wanting to pass judgement here on it he will at least remember that Jesus came to inaugurate the 'worship in spirit and in truth' in which the holy is discovered in the very hearts of human persons.

At all events, since words are not 'innocent', since they summon up differing theological ideas and can lead to breaks in the unity of the Church, it will be understood that it is necessary to be on guard against an ambiguous vocabulary, even if it is in current use in official Church documents.

The Christian Ministries in God's plan

After having thus defined the present context in which we think about the ministries, and having set on one side a problem which is not found in the New Testament scheme of things — and has proved dangerous during the course of the Church's history — we can now make a better attempt at understanding the place of the Christian ministries in God's plan.

St Paul is explicit about the position God gives to ministries in his plan: 'God has appointed *in the church* first apostles, second prophets, third teachers, . . .' (1 Cor. 12.28), and Vatican II recalls this teaching: 'Christ the Lord instituted *in His Church* a variety of ministries' (*Lumen Gentium*, 18). Whether we use the simile of the 'body' or that of the 'house', or again the idea of 'the people of God', in order to describe the Church, every time that we do so we understand that the ministers have their place even among God's people, whether as specialized members of the body (cf. Eph. 4.16) or as stones of the building (Eph. 2.20).

It is vital to emphasize this position of the ministers, within the Church: indeed, there has been at times the temptation to put them above or distinct from the ecclesial community. Now, before being ministers, any who assure a ministry are Christians. Since the example of Jesus himself, who chose the Twelve from among his disciples (Matt. 10.1), the Church's tradition on this point is unshakeable. Let it be summed up in that fine sentence of St Augustine, addressed to the congregation gathered to hear him preach: 'For you, I am a bishop; with you, I am a Christian'.

This fundamental statement sums up all research on the ministries: no one can think about the ministries without first reminding himself what the Church is in God's plan: it is therefore normal and quite significant that the Council Fathers, in the decree on the Church *Lumen Gentium*, preceded what they had to say about the ministries (ch.3) with a fundamental exposition of 'the mystery of the Church' (chs.1—2). As we cannot here sum up the essentials of Christian thought on the nature of the Church, we permit ourselves to direct the reader to these first two chapters of the Constitution *Lumen Gentium*.

This fundamental statement of St Augustine brings in its train consequences which it is important to emphasize. If the Christian ministry cannot be understood save within the context of the Church, neither can those who do not understand what the Church is understand what the Christian ministry is; or they will understand it only in a partial, limited (and so distorted) fashion. At the most they will see in the minister 'the cultic person' or 'the man of God'. . . It would therefore be risky, even at the moment of an *aggiornamento*, to start from the idea of the priest which unthinking unbelievers might have and so to suggest reforms. It is proper, on the contrary, when faced with a serious question of organization or reform of the ministries, that we should have recourse to the opinion of the whole Church in conformity with the practice of the primitive Church (note especially the choice of Matthias, Acts 1.15-26; and the choice of the Seven, Acts 6.1-7).

When we begin to think seriously about the Christian Ministry, it would undoubtedly be a bad method to begin by enumerating various tasks assigned to the minister — tasks which vary in actual experience according to the circumstances. If we try to define what it is that underlies all these manifold occupations, what is essential to the 'ministry', then we are led towards a definition of its function. In trying to think about 'ministries', indeed, it would appear that the Greek word points the way: ministry (*diakonia* in Greek) means 'service', and that word was deliberately selected for the New Testament. The ministry carried no definition in itself, it is defined by its role in the Church, by the service it gives to the whole, by its 'function'. This last word is particularly appropriate; it sums up 'the way of acting, the characteristic role, of one element, of one organ, in a whole'.

Here again the image of the body is very enlightening: the heart and lungs cannot be defined in their own terms; they are organs which carry out a function, circulatory or respiratory, for the greater good of the body. 'If the organ is no longer functioning, illness takes over the body and collapse threatens' (J-C. Thomas, *Eglise et ministères*, Paris 1973, p.131). Ordinarily, of course, we do not give a thought to this or that organ. When one's heart is regularly doing its work, one does not think about it. In the same way, in normal times, we do not think a great deal about the role of the ministers in the Church's life, and yet their function is no less indispensable for the life of the Church. Illness has to strike only one of them for the whole body of the Church to suffer.

This solidarity among the members of the body has been clearly expressed by St Paul:

> There are many parts, yet one body. The eye cannot say to the hand, 'I have no need of you,' nor again the head to the feet, 'I have no need of you'. . . (1 Cor. 12.20-1).

We can transfer the apostle's imaginary dialogues to the Church's members. If the ministries have a particular function within the Church, then Christians cannot say to the ministers 'We don't need you,' any more than the ministers can say to the other members of the Church, 'We don't need you.' There is a solidarity between ministers and other members of the community, as there is between the community and its ministers.

The working of any organ functioning properly in the body ensures the health of the whole body and its harmonious development; so it is in the Church: Christ's gifts

> were that some should be apostles, some prophets, some evangelists, some pastors and teachers, for the equipment of the saints, for the work of ministry, for building up the body of Christ, until we all attain to the unity of the faith and of the knowledge of the Son of God, to mature manhood, to the measure of the stature of the fullness of Christ (Eph. 4.11-13).

If we are going now to try to define the function of the Church's ministers we can once more listen to St Paul:

> Speaking the truth in love, we are to grow up in every way into him who is the head, into Christ, from whom the whole body, joined and knit together by every joint with which it is supplied, when each part is working properly, makes bodily growth and upbuilds itself in love (Eph. 4.15-16).

In this passage it appears that the ministers' functions are described by the idea of 'joints' which allow the Head to direct, feed, strengthen the whole body. Put in another way, the function of the minister is to carry out Christ's role as Head of his Church.

This conception of the minister's function has been very clearly set out by Vatican II, in the decree about the priesthood (*Presbyterium ordinis*): 'Inasmuch as it is connected with the episcopal order, the priestly office shares in the authority by which Christ Himself builds up, sanctifies, and rules His Body' (2); 'as *ministers of the Head* and co-workers of the episcopal order they can build up and establish His whole Body which is the Church' (12).

So we see that the ministry's role is to assure, to signify, to make real the fact that Christ is Head of the Church. This function is sometimes explained by saying that the ministries are the 'sacraments' of Christ, Head of the Church. It may appear a rather technical way of speaking: what is important is to grasp its meaning. It does not in the least mean that ministers replace Christ the Head, which would permit us to imagine that Christ is no longer still the living leader of his Church; but simply that they make visible, they actualize this activity of Christ who gives life, builds, guides, feeds his Church.

To go back to the simile of the body, ministers are not the 'head' for that head is always Christ; they are, rather, the 'joints' — that is, the means by which the head is enabled to carry out its role in respect of the whole body. Or if we try to be more exact in our analogy, our head, our brain, guides and controls the whole of our body, but orders given by the brain only reach the whole body through the nerves and the entire nervous system. . . . Of course we must not try to force this analogy; but it does seem to us to continue the thought of Ephesians 4.15-16.

Such a function is clearly absolutely vital for the Church. If Christ's role as Head of the Church cannot be expressed, then the Church is no longer the Church and will wither away: cut off from its head, a body is nothing but a corpse. Now this function can be lacking not only through the absence of ministers but also because the ministers carry out their responsibilities badly. The Church therefore owes it to herself to be continually vigilant over this, and it will be important to attempt to define how her ministers authentically carry out their function.

If the Church is the Body of Christ, she can be so only by allowing herself to be filled with life by the Spirit which Christ has given to her. Thus the Church is the place where above all the Spirit is active: 'The Spirit dwells in the Church and in the hearts of the faithful as in a temple (cf. 1 Cor. 3.16; 6.19). In them He prays and bears witness to the fact that they are adopted sons (cf. Gal. 4.6; Rom. 8.15-16 and 26). The Spirit guides the Church into the fullness of truth (cf. John. 16.13) and gives her a unity of fellowship and service. He furnishes and directs her with *various gifts, both hierarchical and charismatic*, and adorns her with the fruits of His grace (cf. Eph. 4.11-12; 1 Cor. 12.4; Gal. 5.22)' (*Lumen Gentium*, 4).

This origin of the minstries is clearly shown by St Paul:

> Now there are varieties of gifts, but the same Spirit; and there are varieties of service, but the same Lord; and there are varieties of working, but it is the same God who inspires them all in every one. To each is given the manifestation of the Spirit for the common good. . . . All these are inspired by one and the same Spirit, who apportions to each one individually as he wills (1 Cor. 12.4-11).

This Scriptural affirmation is important: every ministry is a *charisma* (same word in Greek), that is a 'gift' from the Spirit to a member of the Church; not for himself but for the well-being of the whole Church. This 'charismatic' character of the ministry confirms its 'functional' character: no one is a minister for his own sake, but for the sake of others. This fact, however, carries with it a special demand on the Church: it is not the Christian community, in this way or that, which makes its own ministers, it is not the community who provides them for itself, but in whatever way they are designated; the community has simply to recognize them, to discern those to whom the Spirit is offering this gift for the greatest good of the whole Church. Such is the attitude of the Church which, through Peter's mouth, recalls that a candidate for the ministry must above all be a man 'filled with the Holy Spirit' (Acts 6.3). This is also the fundamental meaning of the prayers at the ordination of ministers, prayers which always invoke the Holy Spirit's action, and whose prototype we find in some sense in the Pastoral Epistles.

Hence I remind you to rekindle the gift of God that is in you through the laying on of my hands; for God did not give us a spirit of timidity but a spirit of love and power and self-control (2 Tim. 1.6-7).

The role of the Holy Spirit was strongly reaffirmed by Vatican II; for example, *'through the Holy Spirit who has been given to them,* bishops have been made true and authentic teachers of the faith, pontiffs, and shepherds' (*Christus Dominus,* 2). 'Therefore, *by reason of the gift of the Holy Spirit which is given to priests in sacred ordination,* bishops should regard them as necessary helpers and counselors in the ministry and in the task of teaching, sanctifying, and nourishing the People of God' (*Presbyterium Ordinis,* 7). 'Led, therefore, by the *Lord's Spirit,* who anointed the Saviour and sent him to preach the gospel to the poor, priests as well as bishops will avoid all those things which can offend the poor in any way' (*Presbyterium Ordinis,* 17). This part given to the Spirit is as clearly stressed in the report from the Groupe des Dombes:

> *The Holy Spirit* calls up men and women from among God's people to take on different and complementary ministries, which all bear witness to Christ's fidelity to his promises, and to the richness of his gifts (18).

If we allow ourselves to emphasize this aspect of the Christian idea of the Ministry it is because it has unfortunately been too often overlooked. This aspect brings as its direct consequence the continual need of 'discernment': since the Spirit is the source from whom ministry comes, the Church in recognizing her ministers must be on the watch constantly not to 'quench the Spirit', even though she must always 'test everything; hold fast what is good' (1 Thess. 5.19-21).

This final affirmation leads us now to define some other fundamental consequences of the Christian idea that the function of the ministry is to 'actualize' the role of Christ as Head of his Church.

What it means for ministers

The importance of the role of the ministers is a direct consequence of their function at the very heart of the Church, representing, standing for, actualizing the presence of Christ, Head of his Church. All this is tantamount to their recognizing the authority itself of Christ. The New Testament witness is explicit on this point (see pp. 5ff): Jesus gives the Twelve 'authority over unclean spirits' (Mark 6.7) which means that the Twelve have power to act officially 'in his name'. In another passage in the New Testament this ministerial authority is even more clearly stated, as the decision taken there is more serious; thus St Paul decrees in the matter of the Corinthian guilty of incest,

Though absent in body I am present in spirit, and as if present, I have already pronounced judgement *in the name of the Lord Jesus* on the man who has done such a thing. When you are assembled, and my spirit is present, *with the power of our Lord Jesus* you are to deliver this man to Satan for the destruction of the flesh, that his spirit may be saved in the day of the Lord Jesus (1 Cor. 5.3-5).

Ministerial authority is emphasized once again by Vatican II: 'Bishops govern the particular churches entrusted to them as the vicars and ambassadors of Christ. This they do by their counsel, exhortations, and example, as well, indeed, as by their authority and sacred power... This power, which they personally exercise *in Christ's name*, is proper, ordinary, and immediate. . .' (*Lumen Gentium*, 27). 'Exercising within the limits of their authority *the function of Christ as Shepherd and Head*, they gather together God's family as a brotherhood all of one mind. . .' (*Lumen Gentium*, 28).

If the ministers are wielders of Christ's authority then the other members of the Church must recognize and accept them as such. The need for this, already affirmed in the gospels (Matt. 10.40), had been experienced by the first Christians, as St Paul reminds the Galatians when he writes to them: 'Though my condition was a trial to you, you did not scorn or despise me, but received me as an angel of God, as Christ Jesus' (Gal. 4.14). This is why Vatican II has no hesitation in reminding Christians that 'With ready Christian obedience, laymen as well as all disciples of Christ should accept whatever their sacred pastors, *as representatives of Christ*, decree in their role as teachers and rulers in the Church' (*Lumen*

Gentium, 37). 'In the bishops, therefore, for whom priests are assistants, our Lord Jesus Christ, the supreme High Priest, is present in the midst of those who believe' (ibid., 21).

There perhaps is one of the most disconcerting features of the way in which God's plan works among men; it is a 'communal' plan. 'It has pleased God, however, to make men holy and save them not merely as individuals without any mutual bonds, but by making them into a single people, a people which acknowledges Him in truth and serves him in holiness' (ibid., 9). Ever since then, *God speaks to mankind by particular persons whom he chooses and sends*. The paradox of the authority of the Church's ministers is already, from a certain point of view, that of the Old Testament prophets. They did not hesitate to proclaim, 'Thus says Yahweh. . .', and the people had to recognize this oracle not as this particular prophet's personal idea but as God's idea.

The recognition of the authority of the Old Testament prophets must not have been an easy thing for their contemporaries. It was acceptable only in so far as they felt it that was the Spirit of God who was acting in the prophet; that is to say that every word of the prophets was not necessarily an 'oracle of Yahweh'. We have the same task of discernment when it comes to the Church's ministers: every declaration, every decision of the bishops or of the pope does not carry an equal weight of Christ's authority, and the ministers must spend time in helping other Christians to weigh the import of this or that word, of this or that decision. This does not mean to say that particular actions, particular words of ministers — in particular, the sacraments — do not fully embody Christ's authority; that is the direct consequence of the ministerial function in the Church: to actualize Christ as its Head.

The recognition of the greatness of the ministerial function must not lead any minister to think of himself as a 'superman' or even a 'demi-god' (see Acts 10.25-6; 14.11-15). If the minister wields Christ's authority it must be in the Master's way:

> who, though he was in the form of God, did not count equality with God a thing to be grasped, but emptied himself, taking the form of a servant, being born in the likeness of men. And being found in human form he humbled himself and became obedient unto death, even death on a cross (Phil. 2.6-8).

Ever since then the attitude of the *servant*, of which Christ is the exemplar (cf. Mark 10.45) is therefore also required of the minister; indeed, 'a servant is not greater than his master' (John 13.16). The gospel insistence on this point is somewhat astonishing; it was needed. Indeed, the recurring temptation of those who wield any authority is to take advantage of it in order to dominate other people and more or less directly to exploit them (Mark 10.42). So it is not surprising that Vatican II should have recalled this gospel idea: 'Now, that duty, which the Lord committed to the shepherds of His people, is a true *service*, and in sacred literature is significantly called 'diakonia' or ministry (cf. Acts 1.17, 25: 21, 19; Rom. 11.13; 1 Tim. 1.12)' (*Lumen Gentium*, 24).

This idea of service cannot be in opposition to the idea of authority; quite the opposite. We have noticed above how we are nowadays seeing a change in legal texts which concerns the idea of authority and appears to link up with the thought of the Gospels.

As we move from the idea of 'power' to that of 'authority', the change in vocabulary is indicative of a change of attitude. We have had cause to refer above to the comment of G. Wiederkehr: 'The word *power* calls to mind the Roman *potestas*, which was a right, a power of domination. The word *authority* corresponds to a complex of rights and duties, to what we nowadays call a *function.* . . .' (*Revue de droit canonique*, xxiii (1973), p. 168). If the ministers make certain that a function is continued in the Church, then the power that they wield must not be thought of as one of domination but rather as an authority which they must put at the service of their brothers; its purpose is the general good of the community and not its ruin (see 1 Cor. 10.8; 10.13). Ministerial power is therefore never an end in itself; it finds its justification in the way in which it is wielded in the service of the other members of the Church.

When Jesus sent out the Twelve on their mission, he asked them to 'preach that the Kingdom of heaven is at hand' (Matt. 10.7); and St Paul proclaimed, perhaps in hyperbole, 'Christ did not send me to baptize, but to preach the Gospel' (1 Cor. 1.17)' Thus the first task of the minister, like the Old Testament prophets, is to proclaim the word of God.

The priority of the ministry of the word among ministerial responsibilities is reaffirmed several times in the texts of Vatican II: 'Among the principal duties of bishops, *the preaching of the gospel occupies an eminent place*. For bishops are preachers of the faith who lead new disciples to Christ. They are authentic teachers, that is, teachers endowed with the authority of Christ, who preach to the people committed to them the faith they must believe and put into practice. By the light of the Holy Spirit, they make that faith clear, bringing forth from the treasury of revelation new things and old (cf. Matt. 13.52), making faith bear fruit and vigilantly warding off any errors which threaten their flock (cf. 2 Tim. 4.1-4)' (*Lumen Gentium*, 25).

'The People of God finds its unity first of all through the Word of the living God, which is quite properly sought from the lips of priests. . . . Thus the ministry of the Word is carried out in many ways, according to the various needs of those who hear and the special gifts of those who preach. In areas or communities which are non-Christian, the gospel message draws men to faith and the sacraments of salvation. In the Christian community itself, especially among those who seem to understand or believe little of what they practice, the preaching of the Word is needed for the very administration of the sacraments. For these are sacraments of faith, and faith is born of the Word and nourished by it' (*Presbyterium Ordinis*, 4).

The latter quotation shows well how *Word and Sacraments are inseparably linked*. Indeed, the sacrament is an official and solemn word which pledges the whole of Christ's authority (whence springs our use of the formula 'in the name of Jesus Christ'); the word accompanies an action, of which it reveals the Christocentric meaning. Without the word, the rite practised remains a banal act of everyday living — a bath (i.e., baptism) and a meal (i.e., the eucharist). Only the word which accompanies it can make clear the scope of its link and its union with Christ. Lastly, the sacraments can be thought of as the most characteristic example of the situation in which the word of the minister totally involves the authority of Christ.

On the other hand, the minister cannot invent, nor even interpret without any objective reference, this word of God: he must constantly nourish himself on meditation on the holy Scriptures. These, indeed,

> are able to instruct you for salvation through faith in Jesus Christ. All scripture is inspired by God and profitable for teaching, for reproof, for correction, and for training in righteousness, that the man of God may be complete, equipped for every good work. (2 Tim. 3.15-17).

'Therefore, like the Christian religion itself, all the preaching of the Church must be nourished and ruled by sacred Scripture' (*Dei Verbum*, 21). This preaching of God's word, nourished by Scripture, will normally take place in the course of the eucharistic assembly where the minister is responsible for the actualization of this Word, particularly in the sermon (see *Dei Verbum*, 24; and the constitution on the Liturgy, 52). It can also happen, in a general way, through a commentary or meditation more closely attached to one or other of the books of the Bible, especially those of the New Testament. This was formerly the task of the 'doctors' or 'teachers' (1 Cor. 12.28) of the primitive Church: then it was carried on by the Fathers of the Church among whose writings commentaries on Scripture have a considerable place (e.g., St John Chrysostom, St Augustine); it continued to hold the first place in the old Scholastic tradition: thus, for example, the greater part of the work of St Thomas Aquinas consists of commentaries on different books of the Bible. If this tradition has grown a little weak in the Roman Catholic Church as a result of anti-Protestant polemic, it is being revived today in the form of the biblical renewal and the importance given to the readings and the sermon in the liturgical assembly.

The fact that the ministry is in the service of the gospel entails certain practical consequences. If ministerial authority is in the service of the gospel, it is obvious that it must efface itself in the presence of the Word, and that in no case can the minister by the fact of his authority impose something which is contrary to the gospel. As we have recalled (see p. 27), the New Testament is quite explicit about this: in any conflict, obedience to God's word must be preferred to obedience to the minister.

This conclusion shows very well what are the limits of ministerial authority. If it comes to him from Christ, it exists only in so far as it is being used in accordance with his will. Consequently in so far as the idea of the legitimacy of a minister's authority does not depend solely on the fact of his having been properly invested with it: he must also be wielding it in conformity with the ministerial function in the Church. Here once again we find a link with the modern idea of authority:

> An authority is not legitimate simply because it has been included in a judicial code. . . The way in which authority is exercised has far greater importance than its foundations. (G. Wiederkehr, in *Revue de droit canonique*, xxiii (1973), pp. 175, 178).

God's plan is well described by St Paul: 'to unite all things in him (the one Head, the Christ)' (Eph. 1.10). Consequently the function of the minister, acting in the name of Christ the Shepherd, will be to gather the Christian people into one organic community, into one people of God, to act so that the scattered sheep, listening to Christ's voice, will become only one flock under one shepherd (see John 10.14-16).

The *pastoral function* of leading the community can be carried out, so the New Testament suggests, either at the level of the local churches or at that of the universal Church (Acts 15; Gal. 2). It is, again, well-put by St Paul in his first letter to the Thessalonians:

> We exhort you, brethren, admonish the idle, encourage the faint-hearted, help the weak, be patient with them all. See that none of you repays evil for evil, but always seek to do good to one another and to all. . . (1 Thess. 5.14-15).

The finality of ministerial authority is as clearly affirmed by Vatican II: 'In exercising his office of father and pastor, a bishop should stand in the midst of his people as one who serves. Let him be a good shepherd who knows his sheep and whose sheep know him. Let him be a true father who excels in the spirit of love and solicitude for all and to whose divinely conferred authority all gratefully submit themselves. Let him so gather and mold the whole family of his flock that everyone, conscious of his own duties, may live and work in the communion of love' (Decree on the episcopate, 16).
'The office of pastor is not confined to the care of the faithful as individuals, but is also properly extended to the formation of a genuine Christian community' (*Presbyterium Ordinis*, 6).

In this concern for the bringing to life of the community, the minister will have to pay special attention to the poorer people, following Christ's own example, as the Council again reminds him: 'Although he has obligations toward all men, a priest has the poor and the lowly entrusted to him in a special way' (*Presbyterium Ordinis*, 6). Thus pastoral responsibility of calling together and bringing to life a Christian community is not an easy task, especially today, when in an urban society people tend to regroup themselves according to their common interests or their political views. The problem set by this select-ivity in human relationships which are more developed nowadays than formerly, is very complex. Christians can hold differing opinions on social and political questions, and these are inevitably reflected in the life of the Christian community, whether that is at the level of the worshipping assembly or at diocesan level; nevertheless the minister must always be on the alert not to confuse *bringing the Christian community to life with serving 'any ideology* or human faction' (ibid., 6).

This pastoral responsibility which the minister has must not set him apart from the community. The New Testament lays stress on this (cf. *supra* p. 29); and Vatican II reminds us that 'priests are *brothers among brothers* with all those who have been reborn at the baptismal font. They are all members of one and the same body of Christ, whose upbuilding is en-trusted to all' (*Presbyterium Ordinis*, 9). This means that the minister who is conscious of this solidarity cannot claim to exercise *any sort of monopoly*: the Holy Spirit distributes his gifts to each one as he wills, and the minister has no monopoly of all the gifts just because he has the charge of watching over the whole. In the Body of Christ each member must play his part, and the active participation of every member must be encouraged by the ministers in such a way that they become 'answerable for those who are answerable'.

In considering these few direct consequences of the idea of the Christian ministry, particularly the attitude of the minister and his relation to the community, we have voluntarily confined ourselves to what seems to us most fundamental. Theology's purpose, the purpose of deeper Christian thought, is not to provide a tidy solution to the various problems which arise day by day in the Church's life, but rather to understand what they mean for the faith. Its purpose, then, is to try to state these problems clearly, and in order to do that, to see where they stand and to relate them to one another by reference to the essentials of the Christian faith. Thus we wanted in this chapter to confine ourselves to what appears firmly accepted in present thought on the ministries: in line with this, we have freely chosen to refer quite often to the texts of Vatican II. The idea of the ministry as a function within the Church, a function which consists in signifying the presence and activity of Christ, Head of his Church, and which has its origin in the action of the Holy Spirit, very clearly emerges once more from the constitutions and decrees of the Council; and is rooted, at a far deeper level, in the inspired witness of the New Testament.

It seems to us that such a view reunites in all essentials the ways in which the various Christian churches think of their ministries. However this agreement must not be allowed to mask the different shades of opinion which appear as soon as any attempt is made to go into the details of the consequences which this idea of the ministry involves for ministerial life today. It would then be abnormal to pass over in silence the problems still unresolved; we shall look at them in our next chapter. Quite simply it appears to us very important to emphasize that these problems come 'second', are even 'secondary', and that they cannot be put in their proper place without reference to the deeper, more fundamental approach.

4

WHAT OF TOMORROW?
SOME UNRESOLVED PROBLEMS

The past helps us to understand the present better and to prepare for the future. Our thinking about the fundamentals of the ministry has been nourished by the study of the witness of Scripture and of the texts of the Christian tradition. By the same light we are now going to try to evaluate some unresolved problems in today's thinking about the ministries. The pages which follow form therefore a sort of collection of 'lines of research' into 'disputed areas'. We need not add that even if they let us glimpse new paths or solutions, it is for the responsible leaders of the Church to decide whether to involve the Church in them or not.

The diversity of ministers is an asset which comes from the Holy Spirit. This has already been affirmed by St Paul (1 Cor. 12.4-11) and recalled by Vatican II (*Lumen Gentium*, 12.18). However, when this same Council later lists the official ministers of the Church it appears to recognize only the episcopate, the presbyterate, and the diaconate; and it is again forced to admit that the last has practically disappeared in the present-day Latin Church. Is the Church compelled to form itself around this three-fold hierarchy?

Let us notice at once that the question, put this way, has important repercussions at the ecumenical level. Indeed, if the Orthodox and Anglican Churches have preserved this three-fold hierarchy, the majority of other churches have adopted some other organization for the ministry. So if the three-fold hierarchy were to be required as an absolute necessity for the

Church, unity would be possible only if these Churches were to return to the traditional ministerial structure.

We can now try to answer the question as it has been put by reminding ourselves of a certain number of facts which shed light on this problem.

The principal argument in favour of the three-fold hierarchy is essentially that of Tradition: from the time that we find evidence for the three-fold hierarchy, the ministerial structure has conformed to this model, or — to be more exact — the Church has ordained only these three ministries by using the gesture of the laying-on-of-hands; when in the case of other ministries, the method of conferring the 'minor orders', could vary.

However, this argument might prove to be less restrictive than at first sight. In fact:

— the three-fold hierarchy is only clearly attested from the time of Ignatius of Antioch onwards, from the beginning of the second century AD.

— as Vatican II itself admits, the diaconate vanished fairly quickly in the Latin Church.

— on the other hand, the bishops, and even more the priests, became more varied and arranged in a hierarchy as time went on. We have only to list titles like archpriest, dean, vicar, curate. . . . to see that in fact ministerial structures have evolved.

To sum up, it must be admitted that the maintenance of the three-fold hierarchy down the Church's history is to be found far more in the abstract, or in terminology, than in the actual ministerial structure.

Consequently we may wonder if we must not answer this question in the negative, and all the more because Jesus himself instituted only the ministry of the Twelve, and the New Testament presents us with differing patterns of ministerial structure, but not with that of the three-fold hierarchy. Such a negative answer would indicate that Jesus wants a Church with a ministerial structure, but that the exact form which this takes may vary in different times and places, the unity of the Church being preserved by mutual recognition of the differing ministries.

> The majority of Christians, in the main Churches, are familiar with an ordination of ministers by other ordained ministers, the community taking a greater or lesser part, directly or indirectly, in the choice and approval of the candidates. . . (M. Vidal, 'Ministry and ordination' in *Le ministère et les ministères selon le Nouveau Testament*, Paris 1974, pp. 483f).

No one would dream of disputing that this custom has value and meaning, but the question which can be asked, a question which has ecumenical consequences is to know whether ordination is absolutely indispensable for a valid ministry?

Let us observe at once that such a way of putting the question runs the risk of falsifying our view of the Christian ministry, by centring the problem of validity solely on the act through which the minister is commissioned as such, and not on the exercise itself of his ministry. Now even in today's urban society, as we have seen, an authority is not legitimate just because it has been set up in conformity with the law; it must also carry out the function for which it has been set up.

Indeed the link between ordination and ministerial validity shows itself in history as a very complex problem: 'think, for instance, of the variations, according to period and tradition in the method of judging the validity of an ordination and the ecclesial conditions to which that method is subject' (M. Vidal, ibid.,

(p. 488). If ordination by the laying-on-of-hands is attested by the New Testament, it is not certain that it happened in practice at the institution of every minister: in particular there is no mention of it at the time of the commissioning of the Twelve by Jesus.

Recently the *Motu Proprio 'Ministeria quaedam'* (1972) made a distinction between episcopate, the presbyterate, and the diaconate, where commissioning entails an 'ordination' which includes the laying-on-of-hands, and other ministries where commissioning is carried out without the laying-on-of-hands. This distinction appears to reserve ordination for the important ministries, those of the three-fold hierarchy. St Paul earlier affirmed that every ministry has not the same importance in the Church (1 Cor. 12.28) and this was later echoed by the Schoolmen, who distinguished 'major orders' from 'minor'. The new distinction between ordained and commissioned ministers appears to present the same teaching in different words, but does not offer an answer to our question, at least, not so far as the ministers of the three-fold hierarchy are concerned.

Our backward glance at these few data shows us that the necessity for ordination with the laying-on-of hands and its form seems, to a large extent, to depend on conditions which the Church has decided in the course of her history.

The Constitution *Lumen Gentium* states many times that the 'bishops' are 'successors of the apostles'. This traditional phrase, which seems only to be applied to bishops, does not appear without posing several problems for the historian, problems about the Church's beginnings: the precise meaning of 'successor' and of 'apostle' would have to be determined.

If we may easily say that one bishop succeeds to another in responsibility for a diocese, it is clear that the idea of 'successor to the apostles' cannot be understood in precisely the same way. Every bishop cannot claim to succeed to an apostle's responsibility. We are therefore concerned with a collective succession: the college of bishops at the head of the Church is the successor to the college of the apostles.

But the question comes back again: in what sense must we here understand the term 'apostle'? Are we dealing with the 'apostles' in the historical meaning of the word, that is to say, with those who organized the great missions (e.g., St Paul), or are we concerned with the group of the Twelve, whom Christian tradition has subsequently identified as apostles (see p. 11). It seems that the latter meaning is that of the texts of Vatican II for they declare: 'That divine mission, entrusted by Christ to the apostles, will last until the end of the world (Matt. 28.20), since the gospel which was to be handed down by them is for all time the source of all life for the Church. For this reason the apostles took care to appoint successors in this hierarchically structured society' (*Lumen Gentium*, 20).

Finally, by declaring that the bishops are the apostles' successors, the council before everything else asserts that the bishops today together assume responsibility for guiding the Church as the Twelve did at the beginning in accordance with Jesus's call to them: the bishops' responsibility is thus rooted in the fidelity and continuity of the Church by reference to the primitive Church and to Christ. Under these conditions, there can be little doubt that we must not limit the idea of apostolic succession to the bishops alone, and 'we today happily agree with the reminder that apostolicity must be thought of as a special characteristic of the Church and an obligation on the whole Church, in the succession of all the disciples of Christ' (M. Vidal, 'Apostolic succession and the Church', op. cit., p. 465).

The problem of the ministry of women arises as part of the present movement for the advancement of women in society, and the question is officially 'on the agenda' at the centre of the Roman Catholic Church.

Three arguments have been put forward against the idea of women ministers:

i Ecclesial tradition is opposed to it. For many centuries the Catholic Church has forbidden women entry to its ordained ministries.

ii Christ himself did not choose any women as members of the group of the Twelve.

iii The Ministry implies the exercise of authority in the Church, and such exercise of authority by women is not in accord with God's order of things, wherein women are to remain submissive to men (see Eph. 5.24; Col. 3.18).

These three arguments are hardly convincing:

i Ecclesial tradition is not wholly ignorant of an ordained ministry exercised by women, since deaconesses existed until at least the fourth century A.D. in the East (see p. 45).

ii If Christ did not choose any women to form part of the group of the Twelve, it was because that could not have been accepted by the Jewish mentality of his day; women then had practically no role to play in political or religious life; it is enough to recall, on this point, that according to Jewish tradition, 'in liturgical worship, women were present solely as listeners' (J. Jeremias). We can therefore easily understand that Jesus, while showing himself to be open to new ideas, such as proclaiming the gospel to the Gentiles, (see his conversation with the woman of Samaria) did not want to rush fences.

iii The argument from 'nature' seems to need to be used with care. St Paul was only conforming to the social conditions of his own day: he did not wish to overturn society but to reform relationships within it (cf. the same attitude in thought about slaves in relation to their masters): and in speaking of what is 'natural' we need often to remind ourselves of the French proverb, 'Habit is second nature', and that St Paul was not always taken in by it (see 1 Cor. 11.14-16).

Consequently there appears to us nothing which blocks the possibility of women as ministers; and we have seen that the New Testament bears witness to some unambiguous cases of 'women-ministers' in the Gentile-Christian churches (see p. 35f).

The question of temporary ministries has only recently been raised in the Roman Catholic Church, and up till now has not been especially studied except in the context of the problem of reducing priests to the lay state, and in the scholastic teaching about 'character', based on the tradition of non-repeatable ordinations. To understand it better, we must certainly not confine ourselves to this two-fold approach.

Indeed, the appearance of this problem seems to us linked with the evolution in the exercise of authority in the present-day world. As we have been reminded, people who hold responsibilities for life are becoming rarer in our society. The greater number of such responsibilities, especially political responsibilities, are granted for only a limited period, even if after this lapse of time, they may be renewed. Formerly, things were different; authority was traditionally held for life. In these new conditions, ought not the wielding of authority in the Church, which has hitherto seemed always to have been a life-long responsibility, take this change into account? and cannot we imagine the possibility of ministries entrusted for a limited time?

It is a question which needs to be put all the more because Vatican II itself implicitly raised it by recommending priests and bishops to hand in their resignation on reaching a certain age. This is not yet a 'ministry for a limited time' but it is already the end of 'ministry for life'. It therefore is interesting to stress the justification given for this age-limit: the reason put forward for resigning is they find themselves 'less capable of fulfilling their duties' or 'unable to fulfill their office properly and fruitfully' (*Christus Dominus*, 21-31). This argument comes directly and logically from the Christian conception of the ministry as a function. But then, in a rapidly-changing world, does not the proper fulfilment of the function require that ministers should only bear it for a limited time? Is it not significant that in the Catholic Action movements, structured to the needs of the twentieth century, national or regional officers are elected only for a period? There are some facts in the experience of the Church of our day which call for deeper theological thinking on this matter.